D0397321

THE GREAT STREAM OF HISTORY
A Biography of
RICHARD M. NIXON

by Laurie Nadel

ATHENEUM • 1991 • New York

Maxwell Macmillan Canada
Toronto

Maxwell Macmillan International
New York • Oxford • Singapore • Sydney

PHOTO CREDITS

California State University, Fullerton:
Nixon in first grade, Yorba Linda (Nixon on lower right)

Whittier College:
Senior year, Whittier College football team; 1 year old; Playing violin; With brother Donald; With Donald and mother; As a teenager (age unknown); Lt. Commander Richard Nixon in navy uniform 1945

National Archives:
Ehrlichman, Kissinger, and Haldeman with Nixon; 1969 inauguration; Nixon on phone; Leaving White House August 9, 1974; Smiling; Resignation speech August 8, 1974; 1972 convention, Nixon and Agnew; 1973 inauguration; At China wall, 1972; Nixon with Kissinger

Dwight D. Eisenhower Library:
Khrushchev and Nixon in kitchen debate 7/23/59; Nixon returns from Venezuela, with daughters 5/15/58; Ike and Nixon 8/11/52; Nixon fishing alone 7/29/52; Pat and Dick watch election returns 11/4/52; Ike and Mamie watch Checkers speech 9/23/52

Feiffer cartoons/Credit: Universal Press Syndicate:
Nixon is forever 2/5/89; Now we come to the media 4/15/73

Atheneum
Macmillan Publishing Company
866 Third Avenue
New York, NY 10022

Maxwell Macmillan Canada, Inc.
1200 Eglinton Avenue East
Suite 200
Don Mills, Ontario M3C 3N1

Macmillan Publishing Company is part of the Maxwell Communication Group of Companies.

LIBRARY OF CONGRESS CATALOGING-IN-PUBLICATION DATA

Nadel, Laurie, 1948–
    The great stream of history: a biography of Richard M. Nixon/by
Laurie Nadel.—1st ed.
       p.   cm.
    Summary: A biography of Richard M. Nixon for young people.
    Includes bibliographical references (p.).
    ISBN 0-689-31559-7
    1. Nixon, Richard M. (Richard Milhous), 1913–   . 2. Presidents—
United States—Biography. 3. United States—Politics and
government—1945–   I. Title.
E856.N33   1991
973.924'092—dc20
[B]   90–920

First edition

Printed in the United States of America

1 2 3 4 5 6 7 8 9 10

For Charly and her friends,
especially Tom, Sean, Sasha, and Sam

Contents

Acknowledgments

MANY PEOPLE OFFERED support and encouragement while I was working on this book. There is no room to thank them all. I would like particularly to mention my agent, Madeleine Morel, and my editor, Jonathan Lanman, for their invaluable guidance.

Many thanks to Donna Dees and Dan Rather at CBS News, Jules Feiffer, and Jack Sameth, executive producer of the PBS series "Television." For their assistance in providing photographs, thanks to Joe Dmohowski of Whittier College; Dick McNeil and Mary Young at the National Archives; S. E. Stephenson at California State University,

Fullerton; and Kathleen Struss at the Dwight D. Eisenhower Library.

I would also like to express my appreciation to Simon Boughton, Ana Cerro, Judy Haims, Steve Whitehouse, Sue Watt, Karl and Harlene Brandt, Helen McNeil, Roy Murphy, Rod Bicknell, Judy Cohen, Kathleen McLane, Sharon Weathers, Gil Quito, Maarten and Margaret Van Dijk, Josephine and Michael Brown, Joanna and Sarah Brown, Gillian and Diane Srebnick, Barbara Vettell, Barbara Coats, Vicky Secunda, Shelly Secunda, Julie Zalat, Ray Quezada, Haley Zee, and Louis Railer.

My family has been very supportive. I could not have completed this without the help of my mother, brother, and husband.

In addition to giving me moral support, Jane Finnegan has been my sounding board and alter ego over the years. The combat mentality that characterized the years of the Nixon presidency and the Vietnam War brought us together. Our friendship has grown as we have continued to examine our beliefs and values in the context of a changing political scene. Jane watched and listened while I wrestled with this project, and offered many valuable insights. It was particularly helpful to get the input from her sons, Thomas and Sean, for whom Richard Nixon is just another old fogey their mom and her friend like to talk about.

A Note to Readers

WHENEVER I TELL people that I have written a biography of Richard Nixon for young adults, it seems like I always get the same response: giggles.

If not giggles, then some kind of stifled laugh. Sometimes I notice someone put a hand in front of his mouth to hide a smirk. And the dialogue usually goes something like this:

"Nixon? You're writing a kids' book about *Richard Nixon?* For God's sake, why?"

"That's an excellent question," I reply. When you stop to think about it, Richard Nixon is not your typical American hero. Just the opposite, in fact. He disgraced the office of the presidency of the United States and became the first president in history to resign. In his own words, Nixon "impeached [him]self." As president, Richard Nixon approved plans to commit burglary and secretly wiretap those whose political motives he suspected. He also installed a secret taping system in the White House to record his private conversations. Ironically it was that very taping system that brought him down. Asked how he would handle the Watergate incident today, Nixon says that this time he would burn the tapes before their content could be made public. Hardly the type of behavior to hold up to young people.

Richard Nixon aspired to make his mark on the world in the field of foreign policy. And he succeeded. His diplomatic achievements are the hallmark of his presidency. Many of those who would rather overlook his lies and deception point to President Richard Nixon as the leader who opened the door to the People's Republic of China. And Richard Nixon is still admired by many people who believe that his only mistake was getting caught. Teenagers often tell me that's what they believe, yet according to a recent Department of Education survey, 36 percent of seventeen-year-olds polled believe that the political scandal known as Watergate happened before 1950; 20 percent believe it occurred before 1920. That means more than 50 percent have no idea that Watergate happened within the last quarter century, and thus do not comprehend the impact it has had on our politics and our government.

A troubled, introverted man, Richard Nixon was estranged from his own family as well as his staff. Like the man himself, the Nixon presidency was a mass of contradictions. One cannot easily summarize it as one can many other presidencies. George Washington and Thomas Jefferson were major forces in the creation of the Declaration of Independence and the Constitution. Abraham Lincoln freed the slaves and led the nation through the Civil War. Franklin Delano Roosevelt created programs to provide work and benefits to millions of people devastated by the Great Depression. A polio victim, Roosevelt embodied the courage to overcome personal obstacles. Richard Nixon left an ambiguous legacy for future occupants of the White House and, perhaps more than any other president, challenged our faith in the integrity of the institution itself.

As a college student in 1968 when Nixon was elected president, I was one of the millions of young people who protested American involvement in the Vietnam War. I had a poster on my wall that showed Nixon grinning while his famous shifty eyes appeared to dart around the room. One of the most popular political satire posters of that time, it read, "Would you buy a used car from this man?"

I had first become aware of Richard Nixon when I was four years old and watched him deliver his famous "Checkers" speech on television. I remember my uncle standing next to the TV saying, "How can anyone believe that guy?" As a writer for ABC News during Nixon's reelection campaign in 1972, I screened the incoming film of the Watergate break-in and wrote a story that was aired nationwide. Eleven years later, as a writer for CBS News, I was assigned to produce and write Richard Nixon's obituary.

Although Nixon had nearly died from a blood clot in 1974, he was in pretty good health when I was assigned his obituary. Like all major news organizations, CBS News prepares the obituaries of many important people in advance. My executive producer thought it would be a sound measure to have obituaries of all the former presidents on hand in case any of them suddenly died.

I spent hours screening old Nixon footage, trying to get a sense of who he really was. Again, I watched him shed tears as he described how the only gift he had accepted from supporters was that little dog his daughter had named "Checkers." I watched him sweat and shift his weight from leg to leg as he debated John F. Kennedy. And I watched him give a surly news conference after he lost the race for governor of California—the one in which he snarled, "You won't have Richard Nixon to kick around anymore."

Then I came upon the "Tania" speech. During one of his visits to the Soviet Union, Nixon gave a speech on Soviet television in which he spoke about receiving a letter from a little Russian girl named Tania. Tania, Nixon reported, was afraid that the United States was going to drop an atom bomb on her country, and she was writing to President Nixon to tell him how frightened she was and to ask him not to do it. His voice quivering, Nixon looked firmly at the camera and assured the Russian people that of course he had no intention of dropping a nuclear bomb on poor little Tania.

As someone who had always doubted Nixon's sincerity, I suddenly found myself staring at the monitor. For the first time in my life, Richard Nixon seemed totally credible. At that moment I even thought that *he* believed what he was saying. I realized that despite my own skepticism, millions of Americans had felt this way about Richard Nixon *whenever* he spoke. For years millions of people had been drawn to what they perceived as his strong sense of conviction. Even if he didn't mean what he was saying, I realized, it was his ability to make people believe that he did that was part of his power. Suddenly I understood how people could want to trust him in the first place. What I could not understand was how they continued to do so when so many facts about his dishonesty had been revealed.

I chose to write this book several years after completing the Nixon obituary partly because of my ongoing curiosity about him—the convincing power he held for some, the skepticism if not outright dislike he elicited from others. In the course of working on this book, I found that the more I learned about him the more I was both fascinated and repelled. In trying to understand the forces that molded Nixon's character as well as the major events of his life, I have looked not only at his words and deeds, but also, as much as possible, at his thoughts and feelings. The facts of Nixon's career certainly speak for themselves, but I believe it is equally important to look below the surface at the soul of the lonely man who became the thirty-seventh president of the United States.

Laurie Nadel
October 31, 1989
Brooklyn, New York

Prologue

"FOUR MORE YEARS! Four more years!"

The powerful chant reverberated around the control room of ABC News where banks of television screens broadcast images of crowds raising their fists in salute. "Four more years! Four more years!"

As a writer for ABC News, I was working that election night in 1972, jotting down notes on a clipboard. As the crowd shots changed, creating an eerie, flickering light in the room, I looked at my friend and co-worker Jane Bossler. Jane's face was white, her eyes large and dark with fear.

"This is really scary," she said. "Those fists remind me of Hitler."

She was right. The mood at Nixon's election headquarters was somber rather than happy. Even though the Republican president had won reelection, there was something definitely chilling in the way the crowd kept chanting "Four more years! Four more years!"

None of the people working around us seemed disturbed. "Don't they understand?" Jane said. "Something is really wrong here."

Five months earlier, five men had been arrested at the Watergate apartment and office complex in Washington, D.C., during an attempt to "bug" the Democratic national campaign headquarters. I had written about the arrest and had expressed my frustration at the apparent lack of interest in following up the story. The Nixon White House had played it down as a "third-rate burglary."

"It's a lot more than that," I observed at the time. "Breaking into the opposite party's headquarters to spy on them is a criminal act."

Although the break-in had been reported when it occurred, few Americans realized the far-reaching implications that this event would have. Although few of us realized it that election night, the shadow that hung over President Nixon's reelection had already stretched to include more than just the Watergate incident. In June 1970 the Nixon White House had set in motion plans for its own secret police force made up of agents from the FBI and CIA. This secret police force was authorized to wiretap phone conversations and commit burglaries to protect domestic security. In 1971, after classified documents about American involvement in Vietnam were leaked to the *New York Times,* a White House–sanctioned burglary was conducted to obtain incriminating information on Daniel Ellsberg, the man who had leaked the so-called Pentagon Papers to the *New York Times.* The burglars were nicknamed "Plumbers" because their job was to plug leaks to the press. So concerned were Nixon and his staff about leaks to the media that they went so far as to investigate and wiretap some of their own colleagues. Henry Kissinger, Nixon's national security adviser, had been the first in the administration to start wiretapping his own staff using his own special investigative unit.

President Nixon and his advisers were so suspicious of those who criticized them that they had even drawn up a White House Enemies List. At the top of the list was Senator Edward (Ted) Kennedy of Massachusetts, who posed the most serious political threat to Richard Nixon. Next was Daniel Ellsberg. Other "enemies" included prominent reporters from various news organizations. Keeping the press on a leash was a top priority.

As election returns came in on the night of November 7, 1972, showing that President Nixon had won with an astounding 60.7 percent of the total vote, the victor secluded himself in the Lincoln Bedroom of the White House. There he sat in front of the fireplace surrounded by yellow legal pads, listening to his favorite music, "Victory at Sea." During his first term in office President Nixon had increasingly sealed himself off from his family and friends. His wife, Pat, was concerned and believed that it might have been a mistake on her part to protect and give in to him too much. But she said, "I knew he was busy. The war was hanging over us."

Richard Nixon confided later that despite having won reelection, he had not been as upbeat as he thought he should have been that night. Despite his personal victory, the Republicans had not gained control of Congress, and the war in Vietnam was still underway. He also knew that this was his last political campaign.

But he did not know that his term would be up before the "four more years" he had been elected to serve. Nor did we. Standing in the ABC News control room, Jane and I may have had a sense of foreboding, but we had no idea that President Nixon's second term would prove to be even more alarming and fateful than we could have imagined.

PART I

CHAPTER ONE

The Early Years

RICHARD MILIIOUS NIXON'S road to the White House began in a dry, dusty corner of southern California called Yorba Linda. It was there that he was born on January 9, 1913, the second son of Quaker parents, Frank and Hannah Nixon. He weighed in at eleven pounds and had "a powerful, ringing voice." His parents named him after Richard the Lionhearted. Milhous was the Anglicized version of the name of his maternal ancestors, who had emigrated from Germany to Ireland. The surname Nixon means "he faileth not" in Gaelic, and Richard Nixon would spend most of his life trying to live up to that name.

As a baby Richard was his grandmother's favorite grandchild. His maternal grandparents, Almira and Franklin Milhous, were nineteenth-century pioneers who had moved to California because of its mild climate and cheap, plentiful land. They were drawn to Whittier, a Quaker community east of Los Angeles. There Franklin farmed and invested in real estate while Almira took care of the house and family. Religion played a big part in her life, and she used the traditional Quaker form of speech, addressing loved ones as "thee" and "thou." It was his grandmother Almira who influenced the young Richard Nixon the most. "My grandmother set the standards for the whole family," he recalled. "Honesty, hard work, do your best at all times. She had strong feelings about pacifism and . . . civil liberties. She probably affected me in that respect."[1]

His mother, Hannah, had been raised in that strict but loving atmosphere, with church and school providing her with activities to keep her busy. As a teenager Hannah was skinny and serious-looking. Her nose sloped up at the end, a trait that her son Richard would later inherit. She was extremely religious, even for a community like Whittier. One classmate described her as "cranky and puritanical," while another friend called her "the angel unaware." She had no dates during high school or her two years at Whittier College. It was at a Quaker social that she met a farmhand named Frank Nixon. It was love at first sight for Frank, who immediately stopped dating everyone but Hannah, whom he saw every night.

Frank's mother had died of tuberculosis when he was

nine years old, and he had been sent to live with his uncle while his dad got back on his feet. When his father finally purchased a farm, he sent for the boy. Two years later Frank's father remarried, but Frank's stepmother was cruel and beat him, and he decided to run away when he was fourteen years old, having passed only the fourth grade.

Although he had promised to send money from his first job as a farmhand home to his family, Frank spent all of his farmhand's wages on flashy new clothes. For the next few years Frank drifted from job to job, working as a painter, potter, glazier, carpenter, and telephone lineman. He was argumentative and boisterous, and found it hard to take orders from his bosses. He also found it difficult to stay in one place. After he ran into a car while driving a trolley in San Francisco, he took off for southern California, where he started working as a farmhand again. When he met Hannah Milhous, Frank decided it was time to settle down.

Frank's religious background was considerably different from Hannah's. His people were Methodists and their religious services included singing, sermons, and reading from the Bible. Quaker meetings are largely silent gatherings in which people pray to themselves, standing to speak only when they have something important to tell the group. There are no sermons about hellfire and damnation. Quakers believe in a strong sense of conscience and personal ethics. They tend to behave in a quiet, restrained manner.

To the contrary, Frank was loud, outspoken, and physically affectionate with Hannah, which disturbed Hannah's family almost as much as did his religious background. Her father took Hannah aside and lectured her about marrying someone of her own faith. But despite her family's opposition, Hannah continued to see Frank. They were opposite in so many ways that many of their friends and relatives did not think it would work out. But their different temperaments seemed somehow to complement each other, and four months after they met, on June 25, 1908, Hannah Milhous and Frank Nixon were married. Hannah's sisters and cousins believed that she had married beneath her.

At first Frank and Hannah lived on a ranch owned by her father. It was there that she gave birth to their first son, Harold, in 1909. Three years later Frank took their savings and bought a small lemon ranch in Yorba Linda, a settlement that was made up of "cactus, rattlesnakes, tumbleweeds and tracks," according to one of the Nixons' neighbors. Most of the families moving in at that time were Quakers. They passed laws prohibiting alcohol, dancing, and movie theaters. So morally strict was the town that teachers who worked in Richard Nixon's elementary school were not allowed to dance or to talk to men on the street. The Quaker church was the center of all activity and both Frank and Hannah spent a lot of time there.

Richard Nixon was born one year after Frank bought the lemon grove, which did not turn out to be a great investment. Consequently Richard spent his childhood in poverty. There were many nights when his mother served only cornmeal for supper. Hannah was extremely frugal and managed to save money even when times were tough. So did Frank, whom one cousin described as so miserly that "he wouldn't spend a nickel for a firecracker." When he had saved up enough money to buy a tractor for the farm, he fired the farmhands and did all the work himself. Richard, Harold, and their younger brother Arthur started helping out at a young age. All told, there were five children: Harold was born on June 1, 1909, and died on March 7, 1933, when Richard was twenty years old. Richard was the second Nixon brother, born on January 9, 1913. His brother Donald was born on November 23, 1914, and died on June 27, 1987. Arthur Nixon was born on May 26, 1918, and died on August 19, 1925, when Richard was twelve years old. His youngest brother, Edward, was born on May 3, 1930.

All the Nixons were known as extremely hard workers. They never went to a restaurant or took a vacation, and this early training became the cornerstone of Richard Nixon's personal discipline, a characteristic that would later enable him to push himself beyond ordinary limits during political campaigns.

Like many small boys, Richard Nixon hated to sit still and he sometimes disobeyed his parents. When he was three years old he refused to sit down in a horse-drawn buggy and threw it off balance. He fell to the ground, where one of the buggy's wheels rolled over his head, slashing his scalp. A local doctor had to stitch him up. Another time Richard and his older brother, Harold, refused to listen when their father warned them not to go swimming in a nearby canal where several small boys had drowned. When he did catch them, he hurled them back into the water, screaming, "Do you like water? Have some more of it!" An aunt watching the scene became so distraught that she yelled, "You'll kill them!"[2] But no matter how their dad tried to scare them, Richard and Harold kept swimming in the canal.

Frank was quick to spank his sons and often used a strap. Hannah, on the other hand, never raised her voice. "She would just sit you down and she would talk very quietly and then when you got through you had been through an emotional experience," Richard Nixon said, adding, "We would always prefer spanking." When his younger brother Arthur got caught smoking a cigarette at the age of five, he had cried, "Tell her to give me a spanking. Don't let her talk to me. . . . I just can't stand it." (Arthur had to submit to being dressed in girls' clothes until he was six because his parents had wanted a girl.)[3]

By the time he was six Richard Nixon was a fiercely competitive little soul. His older brother and cousin used that to their advantage by betting Richard that he couldn't fetch something for them by the time they counted to one hundred. "We would bet him that he couldn't get up to the house and bring those cookies or a bottle of milk or something. He'd take off on the run. We'd sit there until we saw him coming. Then we'd pick up the count somewhere in the nineties," recalled his cousin Floyd Wildermuth. Floyd and Harold always let Richard win. "That way, we'd never have a problem with him the next time we wanted him to run an errand," Floyd said.

It was around this time that Richard came home with some grapes that he had picked from a neighbor's vines. His mother asked where he had gotten them and then sternly ordered him to go back to the grape arbor and pay for the grapes with the pennies that he had been saving. Along with such lessons in honesty Nixon learned to imitate his mother's behavior toward his father. Frank often lost his temper with the boys. But while Harold and Arthur would shout back at him, Richard kept his mouth shut, escaping into books and daydreams. At night he used to lie awake next to his brother Donald listening to the sound of a far-off train. "It was the sweetest music I ever heard,"[4] he said, adding that the sound evoked images of other places beyond the tiny, dusty town of Yorba Linda. He would read back issues of *National Geographic* and think about becoming a railroad engineer when he grew up, although when he was eleven he had different thoughts. "When I get big I'll be a lawyer they can't bribe," he said. One of Richard's heroes was a neighbor who worked for the Santa Fe Railroad. Looking back as an adult, Richard Nixon observed that listening to the train awakened his desire to travel. And the argumentative scenes from his childhood, he believed, probably laid the foundation for his lifelong avoidance of confronting people.[6]

When he started elementary school Richard played baseball and football, but he was small and clumsy. He enjoyed music more than contact sports and began taking piano and violin lessons when he was seven years old. But like most boys his age, he wasn't wild about practicing on a regular basis.

Throughout his childhood there was something about Richard that set him apart from the other kids. "He always carried such a weight," his mother said. "That's an expression we Quakers use for a person who doesn't take his responsibilities lightly." Even as a five-year-old in the first grade, Richard Nixon took himself seriously. His first-grade teacher remembered him arriving barefoot like the other kids, but wearing a white shirt, black bow tie, and knee pants. And unlike the other kids, Richard Nixon never seemed to get dirty, she said. By the time he was six he was reading the newspaper and discussing major stories with his father. Perhaps because of his serious manner, "he wasn't a boy that you wanted to pick up and hug," his cousin Jessamyn West remembered. "He had a fastidiousness about him." That fussiness and standoffish quality became stronger as he got older. When he was in high school he complained that he didn't like to ride the school bus "because the other children didn't smell good." Worried about bad breath, he brushed his teeth a lot and would ask his mother to sniff before he went to school to make sure that he did not emit any foul odors. He also demanded that he have a freshly laundered, ironed, and starched shirt for school every day.

Richard Nixon took his religion as seriously as he took himself, which was natural considering its importance to his parents and their community. A curious combination of shyness and confidence may have been part of Nixon's personality to begin with, but it was nourished in Quaker meeting halls, where he was encouraged by his mother to stand up and speak to those assembled. Through the individual silent prayer that was the norm at Quaker services, Richard Nixon learned how to gather inner strength. He did not get a chance to release any feelings through the group singing or praying practiced in other congregations. Consequently he learned how to speak in public, but found it difficult to express his feelings directly.

He did have a great imagination, however, and he loved to write. When he was ten years old he wrote the following letter:

My Dear Master:

The two boys that you left me with are very bad to me. Their dog, Jim, is very old and he will never talk or play with me.

One Saturday the boys went hunting. Jim and myself went with them. While going through the woods one of the boys tripped and fell on me. I lost my temper and bit him. He kicked me in the side and we started on. While we were walking I saw a black round thing in a tree. I hit it with my paw. A swarm of black things came out of it. I felt a pain all over. I started to run and as both of my eyes were swelled shut I fell into a pond. When I got home I was very sore. I wish you would come home right now. Your good dog, Richard.[7]

Psychologists and historians have tried to analyze the secret symbolism in that letter in the hope that it could offer clues to one of the big mysteries of Richard Nixon's personality. Although he grew up in a warm and supportive family, Nixon found it almost impossible to trust other people. Despite the fact that his family and community emphasized the importance of honesty and personal integrity, at some point later in his life Richard Nixon turned away from that. The problem is that no one seems to know at what point he changed.

Throughout his high school years, from 1926 until 1930, Nixon was a straight, hardworking student who often studied past one in the morning. He was known as a bookworm. Some kids called him "Gloomy Gus." Gloomy Gus was a character in a newspaper cartoon who used to go around pessimistically destroying the other characters' fantasies. One classmate remembered that "Dick very seldom came out and played. He was usually studying." Another said, "He was a little different from the rest of us. He was friendly, but not a guy you'd put on a backpack and go fishing with." Like his father, he enjoyed arguing and found an outlet on the school debating team. He was aware that he was not popular and it bothered him. Years later, when he was president of the United States, he spoke about the bitterness he still felt when thinking about his childhood. "What starts the process, really, are laughs and slights and snubs when you are a kid. If you are reasonably intelligent and if your anger is deep enough and strong enough, you learn that you can change those attitudes by excellence, personal gut performance, while those who have everything are sitting on their fat butts."[8]

When Richard was in high school his family moved to nearby Whittier, California, and opened a grocery store and gas station. Everyone in the Nixon family worked there seven days a week. On Sundays they opened the store after church. Hannah Nixon woke up at three in the morning to bake homemade pies that were sold for thirty-five cents each. Richard Nixon used to get up at four in the morning to drive to the produce market in Los Angeles. Then he would drive back to Whittier and set up the vegetables before going to high school. "Boy, I mean, old Dick could peel those grimed-up leaves off the lettuce and tomatoes and make them look like new again," one customer remembered. Richard Nixon looked at his old job differently: "Never again will I go by a vegetable stand without feeling sorry for the guy who has to pick the rotten apples out of it."[9] A $B+$ to A student, he ran his first political campaign in high school and lost to a boy he considered an "athlete and personality boy."[10] As a runner-up, he was made the student government's general manager. The end of his senior year was marked by the Latin club's Roman banquet to which everyone wore togas. Richard Nixon had one of the starring roles in a play produced for the banquet. In the final scene he had to throw himself on the queen's funeral bier. The audience howled, whistled, and laughed. Despite his discomfort at being laughed at, Nixon found that he enjoyed acting.

Although Nixon won a scholarship to Harvard and

wanted to go to college in the East, he settled for Whittier College because the costs of travel and living away from home were too expensive for his family. His older brother, Harold, was dying of tuberculosis and every penny went toward his care. His younger brother Arthur had died of tubercular meningitis when Richard was twelve.

For Richard the hardest part of Harold's illness was not giving up Harvard, but rather having his mother leave home to take care of him in Arizona. In a 1968 presidential campaign film Nixon recalled, "It was a rather difficult time actually from the standpoint of the family being pulled apart." However, Nixon was developing the knack of looking on the bright side of events, no matter how sad or disappointing. "You shared the adversity and you grew stronger and took care of yourself. Not having your mother to lean on, we all grew up rather fast in those years." And in keeping with his Quaker stoicism, Nixon quickly learned to deny that he was disappointed about going to Whittier College instead of Harvard.

Founded in 1887 as a Quaker college, Whittier officially became nonsectarian in 1930, although it continued to emphasize "Quaker responsibility in the social order." At the time Richard Nixon was in college, Whittier's most famous alumna was Mrs. Herbert Hoover, the president's wife. As a seventeen-year-old freshman Richard Nixon kept to the same schedule as he had during high school: up at four to drive to the produce market, back to the store to set up the vegetables, then off to classes. He kept the accounts for the store and studied past midnight. He also managed to get elected president of his class, and president of the Men's Club. He served as a member of the debating team and as a member of the Joint Council of Control (the student governing body), and was a reporter for the campus newspaper, a starring actor in two plays, and a varsity football player. Although he loved playing football, he was too small to be good at it. "We used Nixon as a punching bag," his coach, Wallace Newman, recalled. Even so, Nixon adored the coach, whose motto was "Show me a good loser and I'll show you a loser."

Nixon was considered a "human dynamo" in student government and was willing to tackle jobs no one else wanted. Since he was determined to get a scholarship to law school, Nixon drove himself to get good grades. In his sophomore year he was elected vice president of the student government. It was during this campaign that several classmates remarked on his drive and need to win. In his junior year Nixon was elected president of the student government, having campaigned to get dancing permitted on campus. One of his opponents noted that Nixon had a "tremendous ability . . . to see a situation and take advantage of it."

It was during his tenure as president of the student body that the first cartoons of Nixon appeared. Even at that age his dark, curly hair, heavy jowls, bushy eyebrows, and, of course, his sloping nose made him a delight to caricature. The campus newspaper nicknamed him "Nicky," which he detested. "Nothing is funnier than to call Richard Nixon 'Nicky' and watch him bristle," noted the columnist who had invented the nickname. "I did it once and he was too surprised to speak, if you can imagine Nixon inarticulate."[11] His lack of humor and self-assurance were noted at the time, and he was not popular with the girls on campus. One thought he was stuck-up. Another described him as having "an almost ruthless cocksureness." Many students distrusted his public enthusiasm for school projects, believing that he was putting on a show. As founder and president of a campus fraternity called the Orthogonians, Richard Nixon was already starting to attract followers. Some of his fellow Orthogonians commented, "If this fellow keeps it up the way he is going, someday he will be president."

"Mother, guess what! I have a scholarship for Duke Law School," Richard Nixon's mother recalled his shouting when he got his acceptance letter. Looking back, his mother called that "the proudest day of my life—yes, even prouder than the day Richard became vice president."

Like any first-year law student in a college far away from home, Richard Nixon felt overwhelmed and lonely during his first semester. Duke University, in Durham, North Carolina, looked like "a medieval cathedral town" to the young Californian. He found out right away that the scholarship program he was in was nicknamed "the meat grinder" because it "chewed up" students. Fewer than half of the first-year scholarship students made it to the second year at Duke Law School. To top if off, Nixon found out that there were thirty-two members of the Phi Beta Kappa honor society—a society of individuals noted for their academic excellence—in his first-year law class and he felt he could not keep up with them. He confided his fears to an older student, who told him, "You've got an iron butt, and that's the secret of becoming a lawyer." To his first-year roommate Bill Purdue, Richard Nixon was intense, hardworking, and "not terribly strong on humor." One of his professors described him as competent but "not terribly imaginative or profound." He said that Nixon was "uptight" and seemed to have an "intellectual inferiority complex."

Despite his late nights studying, Nixon continued to feel overwhelmed by his course load. "I'll never learn the law. There is too much of it." Once again his dour outlook and complaining earned him the nickname "Gloomy Gus."

In order to save money so that he could buy his mother a Christmas present, Nixon moved out of the dormitory and took up residence in an empty toolshed lined with corrugated cardboard. A maintenance man who found him studying there exclaimed, "You'll freeze to death!" But Nixon asked him not to tell anyone and the maintenance man agreed. At Christmas break in 1934 he and his younger brother Donald drove to New York City and bought their mother her first fur coat. Returning to Duke after Christmas, Nixon shared a room with another student. He got up at five in the morning to study, then went to class. After class he worked in the library and at other jobs. For entertainment he and some of his classmates went to a boardinghouse that offered all-you-can-eat dinners for twenty-five cents.

During his second year of law school Nixon was elected president of the Duke Student Bar Association and worked on the law review. He also played football and handball, and his extracurricular activities began to take up much of his time. Whereas at the end of his first year he had been first in his class, by the end of his second year Nixon was not doing so well. So concerned was he about his standing that he broke into the dean's office to sneak a look at his grades. As he and two fellow students were passing the dean's office, the others lifted Nixon onto their shoulders so that he could pass through the open transom over the door; then he let the others in and they unlocked the dean's desk where their grades were kept. Nixon found out that he had a $B+$ average. In retrospect, what might have seemed like a simple student misdeed took on ominous implications when information about Nixon's role in the Watergate breaking-and-entering case became public.

During his third year in law school Nixon lived in a cabin in the woods with three other students. Although the one-room hut had no electricity, running water, or toilet, they called it Whippoorwill Manor. Nixon was the first one to get up in the morning. He dressed quickly in the cold so his roommates could have heat later and then went to school where he kept his shaving kit hidden in the library stacks. Retrieving his razor, Nixon shaved in the men's room. He used the showers in the gym. Despite sharing hardships and good times with his roommates, Nixon remained aloof from everyone but his parents, especially his years, nor for that matter from his college or public school years. "It doesn't come natural to me to be a buddy-buddy boy," Nixon explained later, describing himself as "relatively shy."[12]

After graduating from law school Nixon went back home. A job with the FBI that he had applied for failed to materialize because government funding for the post had been cut. His mother helped to get him a job with a local law firm where he handled accidents, divorces, and bill collecting. Nixon lost his first case and was so distraught that he went to Cuba to find out about setting up a law practice there. But said one of his partners later, it was probably the only case that Nixon ever lost in his legal career. Because of his straitlaced Quaker upbringing he had trouble handling divorce cases. He would blush when clients confided the intimate reasons for their marriages breaking up. It was natural for him to seek a specialty that was removed from emotional issues. He began to specialize in tax law and accepted several business clients.

As he had been doing since high school, Nixon put in sixteen-hour days. His long hours were starting to pay off when a group of local businessmen asked him to become president of a company that was planning to sell frozen orange juice, a new idea at the time. After putting $10,000 of his own money into the company, Nixon rolled up his sleeves to cut and squeeze the oranges himself. He attempted to find the right type of container to preserve the juice, but he was unsuccessful. No one knew that you had to distill the juice into a concentrate before freezing it.

Nixon and his partners thought you could freeze the juice as it came out of the orange. Eighteen months after being launched the company went bankrupt and Nixon lost everything he had saved. Twenty-five years later in Whittier there were still former investors in the project who had invested money at his urging and had lost their investment, and who continued to blame Nixon for that failure.

Between 1937 and 1941 Nixon had more success honing his skills in court, where he had a talent for pacing a witness and sensing intuitively that some piece of information was about to emerge. While continuing to practice law, he pursued several extracurricular activities, becoming the youngest member of the Whittier College board of trustees and president of several local companies. In 1939 he became the president of the local chapter of a young businessmen's association called the 20-30 Club. He also served as president of the Duke University Alumni of California, the Orange County Association of Cities, and the Whittier College Alumni Association. Some local Republicans spotted him as a smart, up-and-coming young man, and they began to groom him for political life by sending him around the county to deliver speeches at banquets.

When another young lawyer asked Nixon if he would play the part of an attorney in a local theater group, his first response was to turn it down. The lawyer pointed out that if Nixon did a good job on stage, it would bring him some clients, an argument that persuaded him to try out. He landed the part and at the first night's rehearsal found himself staring at a pretty young woman who was also in the play. Thelma Catherine Ryan was a new high school teacher in Whittier. After the rehearsal, Nixon gave her and her roommate a lift home. In the car he asked for a date. She said she was too busy. After the next rehearsal Nixon drove her home again. Again he asked for a date and was rebuffed. It was during the third ride home that Nixon said, "Someday I'm going to marry you." Thelma laughed her head off. "I thought he was nuts or something," she said later.[13]

As his father had fallen in love with his mother during their first meeting, so Richard Nixon had fallen for Thelma Ryan. But she was not eager to return his affection. The daughter of an Irish coal miner who had nicknamed her Pat because she was born the day before St. Patrick's Day on March 16, 1912, the woman whom Richard Nixon was in love with had, like him, experienced poverty and hardship throughout her life. She was just beginning to stand on her own feet and was not willing to consider giving up her independence.

Pat's mother had died when she was fourteen, leaving her in charge of the family. She awoke at daylight to cook breakfast for her brothers and her dad, then went to school. After school she spent hours doing household chores and working in the fields. (By that time her father had given up coal mining to buy a truck farm in a small California town.) Pat was extremely considerate of other people's feelings and went out of her way to make those around her feel comfortable during difficult moments. Even when she saw her mother's coffin, Pat didn't want her friends to feel discomfort at her sadness, so she put them at ease by commenting, "Didn't she look beautiful?"

Pat Ryan's adolescence also mirrored Richard Nixon's in several ways. Like him, Pat Ryan was active in student politics, serving as vice president of her high school class and secretary of the student government. She too belonged to the theater club and the debating society. A hard worker, she was one of the top students in her graduating class. And their family lives had some striking similarities. Like Nixon, Pat Ryan grew up with a father who had a bad temper, and both of them developed a strong aversion to confrontation. Because of the tension in their homes, both of them chose to escape in their own private worlds of daydreaming and reading. Like Nixon, Pat cherished dreams of traveling around the world someday. They were both remarkably similar in temperament. Having learned to deny her personal feelings, Pat matched Richard's reserve. "As a youngster life was sort of sad, so I had to cheer everybody up. I learned to be that kind of person," she said later.[14] She also learned how to work beyond physical exhaustion, commenting that no matter what, she was never tired or ill.

At the age of twenty-one Pat had driven a retired couple cross-country from California to Connecticut and then had gotten a job at a hospital for tubercular patients in the Bronx, New York. While working, she took a course as an X-ray technician at Columbia University in Manhattan. She was never worried about contracting the disease from the patients with whom she came in contact. Rather, she said,

"They believed they might contract health from me." She added, "That is what gives me the deepest pleasure in the world. Helping someone."

When she was twenty-three she returned to California and moved into an apartment with her brothers in Los Angeles. She became a student at the University of Southern California and, like Richard Nixon, held a variety of part-time jobs. Pat worked in the cafeteria, in the library, at a switchboard, in a department store, and for a dentist. She also landed a couple of parts as a movie extra but found the work boring. She maintained top grades and graduated with honors from USC the same year that Richard Nixon graduated from Duke Law School. She was excited about getting a job as a teacher in Whittier because the pay was excellent for 1937: $190 a month. It seems incredible that there could be such a vast discrepancy between a teacher's salary and a lawyer's. (Richard Nixon was earning only $50 a month at that time. His extracurricular activities, including the presidencies of the local companies, appear to have been done on a volunteer basis with little or no financial remuneration.) Throughout, Pat Ryan was popular with her students and the townspeople of Whittier, who found her enthusiastic, charming, and hardworking.

Although Nixon kept asking her out, Pat kept turning him down and even fixed him up with her roommate. Later she explained, "I thought so much of him that I got him a date with my best friend." She continued to date men she had known at USC. But Nixon would not give up. He pursued her with the same relentless obsession that had marked his childhood and adolescence and would characterize his political career in the years to come. He even went so far as to drive her to her dates, saying that he did not want her to travel to Los Angeles by herself. He would wait for her at the end of the evening and then drive her home. He even took up ice skating to please the woman he called "Dear Heart."

As Nixon had found in his other endeavors, hard work and persistence paid off with Pat. After a while she began taking him seriously. She even got up early to help his mother bake pies before heading off to teach school. (Although he no longer helped his family in the grocery store, Richard Nixon continued to live with his parents. Part of his meager salary went to repay the money Richard had borrowed from his father to pay for law school.)

After two years of dating him Pat Ryan agreed to marry Richard Nixon. Although he had no money to speak of, she believed in his ambition. They got married on June 21, 1940, in Riverside, California, and drove to Mexico on their honeymoon with a trunk full of canned food to save money. As a honeymoon prank someone had peeled all the labels off the cans, so they were never sure what they were about to eat. Ever frugal, they took turns driving so that they would not have to pay for a hotel.

After their honeymoon they settled into an apartment in Whittier for a year before they moved to Washington, D.C. Nixon had been offered a job with the Office of Price Administration, which paid $3,200 a year and gave the ambitious young attorney a chance to see politics at work in the nation's capital. As hardworking as ever, Nixon plugged away at his job, staying in the office till midnight and on weekends. Working that hard not only helped him to excel, but also may have protected him from having to socialize with the people in his office, some of whom were liberals and with whom he felt ill at ease. It was during his OPA job that Nixon began developing conservative views. He also developed a strong dislike for government bureaucracy.

Although he earned two promotions and raises within six months, Nixon was bored with his job writing form letters about wartime tire rations fairly quickly and signed up to join the navy in 1942. As a Quaker, he could have gotten a deferment as a conscientious objector. His government job also ensured that he did not have to serve in the military. But Nixon wanted an opportunity to serve, partly to get away from the dullness of Washington and partly because he sensed that a deferment would hurt him politically later on. Before shipping out from San Francisco on the USS *President Monroe*, Richard Nixon paid a visit to his parents' home in Whittier. There he found that his parents and grandmother were very disturbed by his decision. Nixon said that Quaker pacifism was not effective when dealing with Hitler and the Japanese. Thus his last meal at home before departing for war was "full of sad silences."[15]

As a twenty-nine-year-old navy lieutenant, junior grade, Nixon learned to mix with people from many different walks of life as well as from different parts of the country. He also learned how to play poker, trying out different methods without gambling money for several days. When he felt confident enough he began playing for the pot. When he returned home with several thousand dollars he was embarrassed about telling Pat how he had gotten the money.

Although Nixon participated in one naval landing—the invasion of Green Island in 1944—he did not see combat because the Japanese had already fled. His primary duties while stationed in the South Pacific were to coordinate shipping and handling. It was Nixon who organized and dispatched supplies and food to the field, and he was well liked. When thirty cargo planes once landed with 135,000 pounds of rocket bombs, commanding officer Nixon worked with his crew of nine men to unload the large shipment and transfer it to nearby fighter planes.

Nixon briefed his men carefully about how to unload the cargo plane and transfer the weapons. But in giving instructions, he gave each man the freedom to choose his own best methods for accomplishing the task. The job took five and a half hours, during which Nixon sweated along with the crew, working shirtless in the tropical heat. When they finished he helped them to carry wounded men to the waiting cargo planes so that they could be flown to a hospital for medical treatment. Nixon then went to work as quartermaster, somehow managing to find enough ham so that his crew could get a good dinner.

It was also Nixon's job to censor the men's letters home so that no classified or sensitive information would leak into enemy hands. By reading their outgoing mail he found that everyone was pleased with the ham dinner and nobody mentioned the hours of hard labor in the hot sun. He soon developed a reputation as "a calm island in a storm."

Using his contacts as a quartermaster and supply officer, Nixon set up the first and only hamburger stand in the South Pacific. His talent was in setting up a series of swaps that would eventually get him what he needed for his men. In fact, so legendary were Nixon's exploits in this department that some people have compared him to the wheeler-dealer character Milo Minderbinder in Joseph Heller's famous novel *Catch-22*. He got some supplies from other military bases. Others were "liberated"—exchanged for other goods. "Nick's Snack Shack," as the hamburger stand was called, provided free hamburgers and Australian beer to American servicemen. Occasionally the then teetotaling Quaker even managed to obtain whiskey.

Nixon also began giving informal seminars on business law, in which he taught the servicemen how to incorporate and how to do tax returns. Many of the men who attended these seminars wrote to him years later, thanking him for enabling them to start their own businesses when the war was over.

Popular and respected, Nixon, as before, nonetheless kept a certain distance from others that made it hard for people to get to know him. One of the men who served with him observed, "He was afraid of becoming involved with anyone, even as a friend, because then he would have to reveal something of himself."[16]

Before leaving the navy in 1944 Richard Nixon met Harold Stassen, the young governor of Minnesota who was rising through the ranks of the Republican party. Stassen was on an inspection tour of the South Pacific when Nixon asked him about life in politics. Stassen told Nixon that he would campaign for him in California if Nixon decided to run for Congress. This was the first indication that Richard Nixon was seriously thinking about running for a national office when he got out of the navy, and it appears to be one of the few times that he even discussed politics during his South Pacific tour of duty.

In July 1944 Richard Nixon was transferred to Fleet Air Wing Eight in Alameda, California, where he was joined by Pat. He resumed making speeches at local clubs. After addressing the Rotary Club one night Nixon was approached by Admiral Raymond Spruance, a South Pacific war hero. Spruance shook his hand and said, "Young man, that's the stuff. You're the kind we want down in Washington!" Later in the year Nixon left the west coast for a series of assignments in Philadelphia and New York. Pat accompanied him. He received a citation from the navy for "meritorious service, tireless effort, and devotion to duty," and a new phase of their life was about to begin.[17]

CHAPTER TWO

The Alger Hiss Case

BY 1946 RICHARD NIXON was ready to leave the navy and return to civilian life. Pat was four months pregnant and wanted to go back to Whittier. This idea was attractive to Nixon. After all, he had spent several years cultivating Republican contacts there. Before Nixon left Whittier, the city attorney and a prominent local banker had been among the senior members of the community who had taken a liking to the ambitious young attorney. It was men such as these who had obtained speaking engagements for Nixon at Republican dinner banquets where he was able to build his reputation.

While he was considering what he would do when he returned to Whittier, Nixon received a letter from one of his senior Republican contacts. An old family friend asked if he would be interested in running for Congress as a Republican in 1946. Nixon was delighted, but Pat expressed reservations. Not only would the campaign use up some of the money saved from Dick's wartime poker games, it would also mean a loss of income while he gave up his job to campaign. But Nixon insisted that it was the opportunity of a lifetime and Pat gave in. She demanded two conditions: first, that she never have to make a political speech; and second, that their home life would remain private.[1] Pat said that although political life was not the kind of lifestyle she would choose, Dick had to make up his own mind. When he decided to go ahead Pat promised to help him.

The years after World War II found Americans reassessing their position in the world. Although the Allies had been victorious in that war, they faced the growing threat of communism around the world. The Soviet Union, which was increasing its range of power in Eastern Europe, took on menacing proportions under Joseph Stalin, especially once the Russians revealed they knew how to make an atomic bomb. Meanwhile, the Chinese Communists were gaining ground under the leadership of Mao Zedong. The threat of annihilation by nuclear attack seemed very real indeed. As the Cold War progressed through the 1950s, schoolchildren were led through air-raid drills conducted "just in case" the Russian threat ever materialized. People around the country began building bomb shelters below ground, stocking them with months' worth of emergency supplies in case World War III broke out. Many Americans were anxious not only because they feared that the Soviets would drop the bomb. They were also worried about Communists gaining control of the government and infiltrating the labor unions, which were growing strong by pushing for higher wages for the average worker.

Nixon sensed early that the general level of anxiety about communism presented a good opportunity for him and he quickly took the offensive in his first professional campaign, charging that his opponent, five-term congressman Jerry Voorhis, was a Communist sympathizer. The fact that there was no truth in these accusations did not appear to trouble Nixon at all. In his eyes anything that helped him win the election was valid. This was a belief that he would continue to hold throughout his political career. The drive to succeed was already well ingrained in his personality, but somewhere around the time he left student politics for professional politics Richard Nixon had decided that the end justified any means. He was encouraged in this view by his older Republican patrons, who were desperate to win in 1946 after the death of President Franklin Delano Roosevelt, whose progressive New Deal policies they despised. "The New Deal" was the name given to Roosevelt's liberal domestic action program, which included government-funded labor projects and strong support for organized labor. These Republicans saw FDR's death as an opportunity to regain political control. The GOP establishment had hated the New Deal for its progressive, antibusiness policies, which included strengthening the labor union movement. They believed that New Deal liberals such as Voorhis, who advocated a nationalized banking system, were promoting a policy to turn the United States into a socialist government. That was all the ammunition Nixon needed to charge that Voorhis was a Communist sympathizer who was receiving Communist funds. Although Voorhis was receiving some campaign contributions from a liberal political action committee, he had spoken out against actions taken by the Soviet Union in Eastern Europe and had therefore earned the enmity of the Communist party.

Fired up by the prospect of unseating his liberal opponent, Nixon decided that a no-holds-barred approach was best. One of his high school classmates said, "There was never anything ruthless about Dick when we were growing up. If it was a fair fight, anything went . . . but not anything dirty."[2] But by the time of his first congressional campaign Nixon had apparently changed his ways. One indication of this was his selection of a campaign manager. Nixon hired a lawyer and public relations man named Murray Chotiner, whose reputation for smearing his clients' opposition was well known. Chotiner's other clients included Senator William Knowland of California and Earl Warren, a candidate for governor of California. A fat man with a wicked reputation, Chotiner would continue to guide Nixon through his first few campaigns. It isn't known whether Chotiner or Nixon dreamed up the grand finale to his first congressional campaign, but in the days before the election, registered Democrats received strange phone calls in which someone would say, "This is a friend of yours, but I can't tell you who I am. Did you know that Jerry Voorhis is a Communist?"

The months of campaigning, the financial pressure, and sheer exhaustion created tension in the Nixon marriage. Richard snapped at Pat when she walked in to greet him at a radio studio, screaming, "You know I never want to be interrupted when I'm working!" If Pat's feelings were hurt, she didn't show anything and continued to type fliers, take them to the printer, and stuff envelopes. She also took the mailings to the post office and distributed brochures personally, running home from time to time to take care of her baby daughter, Tricia. She also spent a lot of time offering emotional support to her husband, telling him that he was doing great when his self-confidence dropped after making a speech. This was her first experience as a "volunteer for Nixon," which is how she would refer to herself later in his career.

Nixon's first political victory was the most exciting of his career, and he savored every moment. There were no indications that he felt remorseful over the tactics he had used to win, but several years after his victory over Jerry Voorhis Nixon commented that "communism was not the issue at any time in the forty-six campaign. Few people knew about communism then, and even fewer cared." He also admitted, "Of course I knew Jerry Voorhis wasn't a Communist. The important thing is to win." Later he denied making that statement.[3]

As a freshman congressman in 1947, Nixon felt overwhelmed in Washington. He found himself in the House of Representatives at a time when Republicans were the majority party and he was assigned to the Education and Labor Committee and the House Committee on Un-American Activities (HUAC), which had been set up to monitor and probe alleged Communist subversion of American institutions such as the labor unions. When Nixon joined the committee in 1947 it had already earned a reputation for making flamboyant, unsubstantiated charges against people it suspected of being Communists. HUAC would later become notorious for exaggerating the Communist menace in the United States, a fear upon which Nixon had already started to capitalize. During his first HUAC hearings, on a bill to make the Communist party illegal, Nixon justified his anti-Communist charges by citing a statistic given to him by J. Edgar Hoover, the director of the FBI. Hoover claimed that there had been one Communist for every 2,777 Russians in 1917, when the Communists seized power and created the Soviet Union. But in 1947, Hoover asserted, there was one Communist for every 1,814 Americans! Although no one had confirmed those numbers, Nixon proceeded to base his allegations about Communist infiltration on them.

Nixon used the growing anti-Communist momentum to further enhance his reputation. When HUAC began its infamous hearings on Communist infiltration in Hollywood, it was Nixon who spearheaded the attack, bludgeoning the director of the Motion Picture Producers Association into admitting that although Hollywood had produced some anti-Nazi and anti-Japanese movies during World War II, it had failed to produce anti-Communist movies to serve American propaganda interests. While questioning Jack Warner, head of Warner Brothers studio, Nixon implied that the big Hollywood producers were not as eager to attack communism as they were to attack Nazis because many of them were Jewish. As the sons and daughters of immigrants, many Jews in the late 1940s tended to be liberals who supported progressive policies and strong labor unions. By and large they were not intimidated by the threat of communism. Screenwriters, in particular, were targeted as Communist sympathizers and many lost their jobs as a result of HUAC's naming them as conspirators. Nixon personally handed out subpoenas from the committee to about thirty writers, producers, and actors in Hollywood. During testimony in Washington Ronald Reagan, former president of the Screen Actors Guild, and his fellow actors George Murphy and Robert Montgomery testified that the Communists had not penetrated their union and were not about to take over.

Nonetheless Nixon continued to push for legislation that would set up a Subversive Activities Control Board to determine whether or not an organization was Communist. It would also deny passports to members of the Communist party, who would have to register with the government. In defending his bill Nixon denied that it would lead to a police state. Rather it was "a bill that will prevent the creation of a police state," he said, adding that "we want to expose them, reveal them as enemies of the United States, and deal with them accordingly." Although the bill was adopted by the House of Representatives, it failed to get through the Senate. Years later Nixon acknowledged in his *Memoirs* that "domestic Communism was a peripheral issue" from 1946 to 1948. It was not, however, peripheral to his career. In the first volume of his biography, *Nixon: The Education of a Politician 1913–1962*, Stephen E. Ambrose points out that "although many tried to use the [HUAC] committee to advance their own careers, the historic fact is that the only member of HUAC to ever profit from his association with it was Richard Nixon."[4]

In July 1948 Nixon's second daughter, Julie, was born and he took one month off to help Pat take care of her and their firstborn, Tricia. By the end of that month, HUAC was back in session, investigating allegations that there were Communists in the federal government. President Harry S Truman, a Democrat, had promised that if the Democrats won control of Congress in November, they would abolish the committee. The success of those hearings would determine whether HUAC would continue to exist. For Nixon the months to come would prove to be a dramatic turning point in his career, establishing him firmly as a national political figure.

The first person to testify before the new session of the House Committee on Un-American Activities on July 31, 1948, was a woman who claimed that she had been a courier, or messenger, for the Communist party in the 1930s and 1940s. She named several names and claimed to have reported them to the Justice Department several years earlier. Nixon made a point of saying that the Truman administration had failed to act on this information. Whittaker Chambers, a former State Department employee and a confessed former Communist party member, was called to the stand to corroborate the courier's testimony. On August 3, Chambers made headlines around the world when he stated that he had belonged to an "underground cell" of government employees who were members of the Communist party. In naming them, Chambers singled out Alger Hiss, who was at that time president of the Carnegie Endowment for International Peace. He also said he had informed the FBI about the Communist cell as early as 1943.

Alger Hiss cabled the committee and requested an appearance to refute Chambers's charges. A tall, elegant man with impeccable credentials that included friendships with the secretary of state and other government leaders, Hiss read a statement denying that he had ever been a member of the Communist party. He said that he had never heard the name Whittaker Chambers and, when shown a photograph, that he had never seen him before. Hiss was quick to add, "I would not want to take oath that I had never seen that man," asking, "Is he here today?" When told no, Hiss appeared disappointed.

It was at that moment that Congressman Nixon's experience as a poker player and as a courtroom lawyer became extremely useful. Nixon knew that when Hiss denied knowing Chambers he was actually bluffing. He also noticed that Hiss hedged a lot and not once did he actually say outright that he did not know Chambers. Even more revealing to Nixon was the way Hiss seemed to be overreacting on the witness stand. Nixon was also aware that rumors about Hiss's Communist background had circulated through the nation's capital for years. However, no one had come up with any evidence. Since Hiss had been a member of the State Department and a trusted adviser under President Roosevelt, the Democrats did not want to be embarrassed by any public revelations concerning his affairs. When the rumors had surfaced in the mid-1940s the Democrats had moved him out of his job at the State Department without making a big deal about it.

But for now Nixon had nothing more than his hunch to go on. Without facts to back up Chambers's claims Nixon could not push for Hiss's trial and conviction. In fact the Hiss case was so controversial that Nixon was warned by several senior congressmen that it could cause the committee's downfall. The committee's credibility was already being undermined by gossip that Whittaker Chambers was a drunken, insane homosexual. Nixon believed it was incumbent upon him to prove definitively that Whittaker Chambers was right and that Alger Hiss had indeed been a member of the Communist party during his tenure as a State Department official.

To make the committee's job harder, President Truman had prohibited all federal government offices from giving information about their employees to any congressional committee. So Nixon took a different tack. He told his fellow HUAC members that they did not have to prove that Alger Hiss was a Communist. All they had to do was show that Hiss had lied when he denied having known Whittaker Chambers. Nixon was given the task of interrogating Chambers in the face of growing public disbelief in his star witness. Later Nixon would refer to this part of the Alger Hiss case as his first real test. He was attacked by the press and became the subject of sniping editorial cartoons. Despite his doubts Nixon believed that ultimately he would be proved right.

In order to nail down Chambers's testimony Nixon asked him whether Hiss had any hobbies that only close personal friends would know about. Chambers gave him some quirky bits of personal information. Hiss and his wife were bird watchers. They drove an old black Ford. Chambers knew some details about the Hisses that indicated that he had indeed known them personally, and he said he would take a lie detector test to prove he was telling the truth.

In the meantime Nixon sent his staff scurrying around Washington looking for any papers that would link Chambers with Hiss. He drove down to Chambers's farm in Westminster, Maryland, in the hope of turning up fresh evidence of a link between the two men. He spent a lot of time with Chambers, whose children began calling the young congressman "Nixie the kind and the good." But apart from learning that Alger Hiss's wife was a Quaker, Nixon did not get the material he was looking for.

After another round of hearings it became clear to him that although Whittaker Chambers was answering every question put to him, he was not offering any information. It also became clear to him that Chambers was holding something back. But until he and his colleagues could find out what that was, the members of HUAC themselves remained at the center of a public storm. So fierce was the criticism of them that Nixon's parents became worried that the case would ruin his career. They asked him to stop pursuing Alger Hiss, pointing out that older, more experienced members of the House and the Senate had asked him to stop too. Nixon said, "Mother, I think Hiss is lying. Until I know the truth, I've got to stick it out." He insisted, "If the American people understood the real character of Alger Hiss, they would boil him in oil."[5]

Alger Hiss was called again to the witness stand, and as he began to stumble, more members of the committee began to share Nixon's view. One committee member told Hiss, "Whichever one of you is lying is the greatest actor that America has ever produced." In order to smoke out the answer to that one, Nixon called for a public hearing in which Hiss and his accuser, Chambers, would go face to face.

"Mr. Hiss, the man standing here is Mr. Whittaker Chambers. I ask you now if you have ever known that man before," Congressman Nixon demanded. Hiss did not answer but asked Chambers to speak and to read a passage from a magazine, claiming that he wanted to hear his voice before attempting an identification. Then he demanded to see Chambers's teeth, insisting on the name of his dentist. Nixon curtailed this distracting discussion by insisting that Hiss speak directly to Chambers. Hiss asked whether Chambers had visited Hiss's apartment and Chambers said, "I most certainly did," adding "I was a Communist and you were a Communist." It was then that Hiss confessed by announcing, "The ass under the lion's skin is George

Crosley. If he had lost both eyes and taken his nose off, I would be sure." George Crosley had apparently been Chambers's cover name. Nixon asked Chambers to confirm that he knew the man in front of him. "Positive identification," said Chambers. Nixon knew he had Hiss cornered.

Although Nixon had been instrumental in proving that the two men knew each other, he continued to work around the clock to get more evidence against Hiss. He stopped sleeping and was finally ordered by another congressman to take a sleeping pill. At the next round of the Hiss hearings Nixon kept Hiss on the witness stand for five hours, ferreting out facts and dates that supported Chambers's position that the two men had known each other during their Communist years. Hiss claimed, "The important charges are not questions of leases, but questions of whether I was a Communist." Nixon replied, "The issue in this hearing today is whether or not Mr. Hiss or Mr. Chambers has committed perjury before this committee, as well as whether Mr. Hiss is a Communist." As a lawyer, he knew he needed to keep the committee focused on all possible charges. Later Chambers took the stand and testified that he held no personal grudge against Hiss. "We were close friends, but we are caught in a tragedy of history," Chambers said. After the hearing Hiss countered by filing a $50,000 lawsuit against Chambers, saying that Chambers's accusations had ruined his reputation.

The November 1948 elections proved to be a stunning upset for Republicans, who expected their candidate Thomas Dewey to defeat Harry Truman for the presidency.

Describing himself as "unpleasantly surprised" by the results, Nixon now found himself in a Congress controlled by Democrats, and he believed that would spell doom for the House Committee on Un-American Activities and the Hiss hearings. (That hunch would turn out to be false. HUAC continued to operate with a Democratic majority.) Nixon had put a lot of energy into campaigning for the Republicans, and he had made a big deal out of the Hiss case and the Communist menace in general. He was so depressed when the Republicans lost that he decided it was time to go on vacation. He had not taken one in two years. He and Pat booked a cruise to Panama and he assured her that "absolutely nothing" would stop them from going.

On December 1, 1948, just before they were set to leave, two contradictory accounts of the Hiss case appeared in the press. A United Press report in the *Washington Daily News* said that the Justice Department was going to drop its investigation of both Hiss's and Chambers's alleged perjury unless more evidence was forthcoming. The *Washington Post* reported that "some very startling information on who's a liar" had been uncovered in connection with the case.

Apparently Hiss's lawyers had asked Chambers whether he could provide documents to substantiate his charges against Hiss. Chambers brought forth sixty-five papers that he claimed Hiss had stolen from the State Department while he was working there. Chambers further claimed that Hiss had told Chambers to deliver those papers to a Soviet agent. This meant that Chambers had perjured himself by telling HUAC that neither his nor Hiss's Communist party group had actually spied. It also meant that Hiss would now face charges of treason as well as perjury.

Nixon was peeved that his star witness had delivered the evidence to the Justice Department and not to him, the committee, or the FBI. "I'm so goddamned sick and tired of this case. I don't want to hear any more about it and I'm going to Panama. And the hell with it, and you, and the whole damned business!" he raged at a fellow committee member. But when urged to visit Chambers's farm one last time Nixon gave in.

At the farm Chambers told Nixon that he had turned over the papers when asked about them by Hiss's lawyer. The lawyer in turn had given them to the Justice Department. Nixon couldn't believe that Hiss's lawyers had been holding the evidence for two weeks and believed that the Justice Department had leaked the story about dropping the case. He called Chambers stupid for giving away the documents. It was then that Chambers confessed, "I have another bombshell in case they try to suppress this one."

For some reason, possibly exhaustion, Nixon failed to act at that critical moment. He could have served Chambers with a subpoena ordering him to hand over those documents right then and there. Instead he blurted to his companion, "I don't think he's got a damned thing. I'm going right ahead with my plans." After all, he said, he couldn't disappoint Pat by canceling their vacation. However, another committee member ordered Nixon to have Chambers's new evidence subpoenaed immediately. He put the machinery in motion, then left on his cruise.

While he and Pat were at sea, two members of HUAC were dispatched to Chambers's farm. When they arrived he led them to a pumpkin patch in a corner of his field. From the inside of a hollowed-out pumpkin Chambers lifted out microfilm of State Department files in Hiss's handwriting. The documents, which were immediately dubbed "the pumpkin papers," dated as far back as the 1930s.

Pat and Richard Nixon were dining at the captain's table when the telegram arrived: SECOND BOMBSHELL OBTAINED BY SUBPOENA. "Here we go again!" sighed Pat as her husband radioed to shore for special transportation back to the States. He was picked up by military transport and flown to Miami, where once again the young congressman from California made headlines. Pat stayed behind on the ship and went home alone after the cruise ended.

Now the case was hotter than ever. Chambers had obviously been involved in espionage along with Hiss. Otherwise, how could he have obtained the pumpkin papers in the first place? And since Chambers had perjured himself by denying that he had done any spying, how could he be trusted when he said that Hiss had given him the documents to be turned over to a Russian agent? Chambers was obviously guilty of spying. The way Nixon read the situation, the Justice Department would indict Chambers rather than Hiss, and that in itself would be enough to destroy Nixon's political career. After all, he had been the one ruthlessly pursuing Hiss solely on the basis of Chambers's testimony. It was Chambers who possessed the documents that proved espionage had been committed. There were no papers in

Hiss's possession. He was connected to the case through Chambers's verbal accusations.

Yet another bombshell exploded when Nixon examined the numbers on the microfilm and called Eastman Kodak to verify them. It turned out that the microfilm had been made in 1945. Chambers had told them he had used the microfilm to copy the State Department documents in 1938 after he pulled out of the Communist party. Shocked and alarmed by yet more proof that Chambers was a liar, Nixon began to cry, "Oh my God, this is the end of my political career." He cursed his staff and demanded that they do something to save the situation. Then he called Chambers and asked him whether he had indeed microfilmed the documents in 1938. Chambers said yes and Nixon told him that the film had not been manufactured until 1945. Chambers replied, "I can't understand it. God must be against me."

Nixon became furious and told him, "You'd better have a better answer than that!" Shortly after Chambers got off the phone he tried to commit suicide. Around the same time Eastman Kodak called Nixon to say that they had double-checked and that the microfilm had been manufactured in 1937. Nixon's mood shifted immediately from black fury to elation. "Poor Chambers," he commented. "Nobody ever believes him at first."[6] But nobody in Nixon's office thought to phone the distraught Chambers to let him know that he had been vindicated.

Further investigation turned up the typewriter that Priscilla Hiss had used to type copies of those State Department documents that Chambers had microfilmed and stuffed into the pumpkin. The letters on the typewriter and the pumpkin papers matched exactly. Upon being shown the evidence at a grand jury hearing Hiss commented, "Until the day I die, I shall wonder how Whittaker Chambers got into my house to use my typewriter." Everyone in the room laughed. Then the grand jury ruled to indict Hiss for perjury. They could not indict him for espionage because of a three-year statute of limitations.

The Hiss case had begun in August and ended in December 1948. With the case behind him Nixon was riding high. His reputation as a commie basher was gaining him support around the country. In fact it was during the Alger Hiss hearings that a young student at the University of California at Los Angeles named H. R. (Bob) Haldeman first began to worship him. Haldeman, whose right-wing views included a strong belief that the Communists were penetrating vital American institutions, would eventually latch on to Nixon's campaign and become his most trusted adviser as well as his obsessive protector. For his part, Richard Nixon was unaware of Haldeman's existence as the Hiss trial concluded. He was aware that his strong-arm tactics were effective and popular. He had been tested in crisis and believed that he functioned well under stress despite his flashes of temper. Once again Nixon had adhered to a pattern of obstinate persistence in the face of extreme opposition and it had paid off. He had gambled that Hiss was guilty and he had won. Now he was ready for another challenge.

CHAPTER THREE

Tricky Dick

IT WAS TIME for Richard Nixon to cash in on his newfound recognition. The young congressman quietly began preparing to run for the United States Senate. He rehired Murray Chotiner as his campaign manager and prayed that the jury would convict Alger Hiss so that he could ride into office on the momentum.

On November 3, 1949, Nixon officially announced his Republican candidacy for senator from California in the 1950 election. Two months later he got his wish regarding Hiss, and soon found himself besieged by congratulatory cables. Now he could really play on the public's fear of communism in his campaign speeches. "This nation cannot afford another Hiss case," was one of his standard lines. At the same time that he capitalized on his involvement with the Hiss case by appealing to those who shared his views, he also used it to his advantage by maintaining that he was being persecuted politically by those who opposed his point of view and implied that this was because they themselves were Communist sympathizers.

In the California primary Nixon chose to cross-file, which meant that he could run as both a Democrat and a Republican. Although technically Nixon was campaigning as a candidate for both parties in the primary, his affiliation was with the Republican party and he should properly have indicated to voters that his decision to cross-file did not make him a Democrat. Rather it enabled him to take advantage of a common political practice at the time. In order to gain supporters the Nixon campaign distributed a pamphlet called *As One Democrat to Another*. The pamphlet showed pictures of Nixon and his family and Nixon in the navy. It portrayed Nixon as a war hero and went on to talk about his role in the Alger Hiss case. Because of its title and the fact that the pamphlet never actually said that Nixon was a Republican, it served to confuse many voters who voted for him believing that he was a Democrat. The *Los Angeles Times*, however, did point out that considering Congressman Nixon's "antipathy to perjury," the pamphlet was a "deceitful device."

The pamphlet was believed to have been Chotiner's idea, as was the establishment of committees called "Democrats for Nixon." Some of these committees were simply fronts that Chotiner and Nixon's fund-raiser set up to make people think that Nixon had widespread Democratic support. However, some were genuine, set up by conservative Democrats who believed that the Communists constituted a genuine threat to America.

After winning the Republican primary Nixon faced off against his Democratic opponent, Congresswoman Helen Gahagan Douglas, whose husband, Melvyn Douglas, was a famous movie actor. At the time Ronald Reagan, later to become president himself, was the head of the Screen Actors Guild and a member of the Democratic Party. He backed Douglas.

Many of her detractors claimed that Douglas was what is sometimes derogatorily referred to as a "bleeding-heart liberal." As a supporter of FDR's New Deal, Douglas advocated subsidized housing for the poor, angering wealthy real estate dealers and developers. Her opposition to funding the House Committee on Un-American Activities further contributed to her earning the "bleeding heart" nickname. Because she was a woman in a predominantly male field she was mistrusted by her colleagues and often made the subject of male chauvinist jokes. Senator John F. Kennedy, Democrat of Massachusetts, also later to become president, was among those who did not believe she belonged in politics. He surprised Nixon one day by walking into his office with a $1,000 campaign contribution, saying that although he could not endorse Nixon's candidacy, he wanted to help out.[1]

In February 1950 Senator Joseph McCarthy, Republican of Wisconsin, gave a historic speech. The previous autumn Mao Zedong and his troops had come to power, creating the People's Republic of China. McCarthy claimed that he had the names of Communists in the State Department who had caused China to become a Communist regime. Also in the fall of 1949 the Soviets tested an atom bomb, an event which McCarthy claimed could only have happened because of Communists working on the United States government's top-secret atom bomb project. Considered one of the most conservative members of Congress at that time, McCarthy had not played a role during the Alger Hiss hearings because he was a senator and the hearings took place in the House of Representatives. When he did emerge, however, McCarthy made news with his claims that he had the names of Communists—nicknamed "reds" because of the red Communist flag—inside the government.

McCarthy's name became associated with the phrase "red scare" almost instantly. He was so blatant that Nixon appeared subtle by comparison. Even though Nixon distorted Douglas's voting record and implied that she was a Communist sympathizer, this comparison worked to Nixon's advantage in his campaign. In response Douglas issued a pamphlet that said, "The Big Lie. Hitler invented it. Stalin perfected it. Nixon uses it." She tried to emphasize comparisons between Nixon and Senator McCarthy, although the two were operating independently. Murray Chotiner then devised a number of quick smears to use against

Douglas. Nixon began calling her "the pink lady" and said that she was "pink right down to her underwear." Douglas started calling him "Tricky Dick," a name that would haunt him throughout his career. In the final hours of the campaign Nixon workers organized a phone drive in which they offered voter incentives in the form of electric clocks, Silex coffeemakers, and toasters to all who said they would vote for Nixon.

All those unsavory tactics worked and Richard Nixon celebrated his Senate victory by going from party to party playing "Happy Days Are Here Again" on various pianos. (He had studied piano as a child.) But his victory, at the end of a dirty campaign, left a bitter taste in many people's mouths. For years after Nixon won the Senate election Helen Gahagan Douglas's husband would leave the room whenever Nixon's name was mentioned.

Never a man to sit still, Nixon used his position as senator to expand his base within the Republican party. He became an after-dinner speaker at Republican events around the country and refused to accept money for those speeches. Soon a lot of Republicans owed him favors, which meant that he was building a solid "bank" of supporters that he would be able to call on in later years. In 1951 he spoke in twenty-five states, making about three speeches a week. Often he insisted that Pat come with him even though she preferred to stay home. Julie and Tricia often cried as she hugged them good-bye, and Pat said that she felt guilty about leaving them with baby-sitters. She disliked attending political functions altogether and did so only out of devotion to her husband. (On those rare occasions that he was home with Pat and his two young daughters, Nixon would play "Some Enchanted Evening" on the piano while his wife sewed, read, or baked cakes.)[2]

Whatever the cost to his family, spending three or four nights a week away from home soon paid off as Nixon's name started coming up in connection with the 1952 presidential campaign. As a result of the United States's unsuccessful involvement in the Korean War, President Truman was becoming increasingly unpopular. Although Nixon was too inexperienced to be considered a contender for the presidency, his name was still among those circulating. Senator Robert Taft appeared to be the front-runner until General Dwight D. Eisenhower, the much admired commander of the Allied forces during World War II, joined the race. Although Taft was a long-standing Republican and a professional politician with broad support among the Republican establishment, war hero Eisenhower was far more popular with the public at large. At first Nixon practically worshiped Eisenhower because of the general's accomplishments during the war. The young senator described Eisenhower as "erect and vital and impeccably tailored." He also believed that Eisenhower knew more about foreign policy than any of the other candidates. When the two men first met Nixon even found that he could relax because of Eisenhower's natural warmth and sincerity. For his part, Eisenhower was impressed by Nixon's seriousness and by his hard work during the Hiss case. "The thing that most impressed me was that you not only got Hiss, but you got him fairly," Eisenhower told Nixon. He also expressed admiration for Nixon's conservative views.[3]

Although the presidency was out of the question for Nixon, the vice presidency might not be, and as Nixon began maneuvering himself into position with Eisenhower he quickly offended Taft's supporters. As the number-two contender for the Republican presidential nomination, Taft would naturally have been the most likely choice as Eisenhower's running mate. But the young upstart Nixon had upstaged the senior Republican. Behind his back Nixon was being called "a little man in a big hurry." Even some fellow Republicans were now calling him "Tricky Dick."[4]

By the summer of 1952 it looked like Nixon would be Eisenhower's choice, and that prospect was creating tension between him and Pat. The night before the Republican convention in Chicago, Illinois, Nixon had to spend several hours trying to convince Pat that his running for vice president was a good idea. She was vehemently opposed. Nixon was about to give up the race when he called Murray Chotiner. Chotiner talked him back into it and Nixon went back to work on persuading Pat. It was five in the morning when his wife surrendered. "I guess I can make it through another campaign," she said.

Richard Nixon was thirty-nine years old and had only been in politics for six years when he was chosen as the vice-presidential candidate. Pat was rushed from her hotel suite to the victory podium where she kissed him on the cheek. Without even looking at her Nixon put one hand around her shoulder and used the other to shake his supporters' hands. He and Eisenhower posed for photographers while the band played and cheering swept the hall. Nixon took the microphone and said, "Haven't we got a wonderful candidate for president of the United States?" The crowd went wild.

Arriving home after the convention, Pat and Richard Nixon told their children that Daddy would be running for vice president of the United States, and that if he won he would be helping the president. But six-year-old Tricia simply groaned. "You mean that you're going campaigning again?"[5]

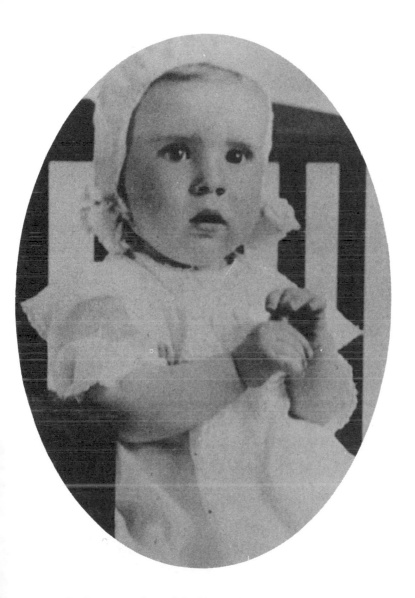

The future president of the United States at one year old
(WHITTIER COLLEGE)

Richard Nixon is on the lower right in this picture of his first-grade class.
(CALIFORNIA STATE UNIVERSITY, FULLERTON)

Donald (on left) and Richard (on right) with their mother Hannah Nixon
(WHITTIER COLLEGE)

Richard Nixon with violin
(WHITTIER COLLEGE)
Richard Nixon (on left) with his brother
Donald *(WHITTIER COLLEGE)*

Richard Nixon as a teenager
(WHITTIER COLLEGE)

Richard Nixon (top row, center) was a senior at Whittier College and a member of the football team in 1933.

(WHITTIER COLLEGE)

Lieutenant Commander Richard Nixon in his navy uniform, 1945 (WHITTIER COLLEGE)

CHAPTER FOUR

Checkers

RICHARD NIXON HIT the campaign trail with both fists swinging. He attacked the Truman administration for failing to move against Alger Hiss, warning that for each Alger Hiss uncovered in the United States there lurked ten undiscovered scandals in the Truman government. Nixon also charged that 600 million people had gone over to communism since Harry Truman had become president, referring to the Communist takeover of mainland China. Nixon began to portray himself as a twentieth-century Abraham Lincoln. In many of his speeches he stressed his poor background and told voters how he drove a used car and had big mortgage payments to make. At the same time he criticized those government officials who accepted expensive gifts in exchange for favors. By creating an image of himself as "Poor Richard," Nixon was telling Americans that he had problems making ends meet just as they did.

In September 1952 stories that Richard Nixon allegedly received between $16,000 and $20,000 a year in supplemental income began to surface in the media, contradicting the image he was building and raising questions about Nixon's financial ethics. When questioned, Nixon said that the supplemental fund was in fact for campaign expenses. On September 18, however, the *New York Post* ran a front-page story with the headline SECRET NIXON FUND! "Secret Rich Men's Trust Fund Keeps Nixon in Style Far beyond His Salary," the subhead said. Despite the hints at improper financial influence over the vice-presidential candidate, Nixon's campaign manager, Murray Chotiner, dismissed the story as "a tempest in a teapot."

But the following day Nixon's secretary, Rose Mary Woods, was besieged by phone calls and cables, some of them calling for Nixon to resign from the campaign. Other newspapers picked up the story. One called Nixon "the pet and protégé"[1] of rich Californians. (He was still being supported by California businessmen.) The Democrats began calling for Nixon's resignation and, privately, some of Eisenhower's advisers said that wasn't such a bad idea. As far as they were concerned, the young senator from California was too extreme in his anticommunism and they believed he would hurt Eisenhower at the polls. But another group of Eisenhower's men saw it differently. If Nixon resigned, then voters would think that Eisenhower had chosen a crook as his running mate and would lose confidence in him.

Nixon took the offensive, accusing the Democratic vice-presidential candidate, John Sparkman, of putting his wife on the government payroll whereas Pat Nixon put in long hours but took no money from taxpayers. "The purpose of these smears is to make me, if possible, relent in my attacks on the Communists and the crooks in the present administration," Nixon said. "The more they smear me the more I'm going to expose the Communists and the crooks and those who defend them until they throw them all out of Washington."[2]

Newspaper editorials continued to flow thick and fast, but General Dwight D. Eisenhower withheld comment. This hurt Nixon and made him angry. He thought that Eisenhower, popularly known as Ike, should take a public stand for him. In fact Eisenhower had written a letter suggesting to Nixon that he submit to an investigation by the Senate Committee of Ethics in Government. But he never sent that letter, having decided that Paul Douglas, the Democratic senator who chaired the committee, would not be fair to a Republican vice-presidential candidate. Instead Eisenhower went public with a statement of support: "I believe Dick Nixon to be an honest man. I am confident that he will place all the facts before the American people fairly and squarely." He said that he planned to speak to Nixon "at the earliest time," but then made sure that he was inaccessible for the next few days. If Eisenhower was being diplomatic, the reporters covering him were blunt. They took a poll among themselves and voted forty to two for Ike to dump Nixon. Eisenhower called the reporters in and said that he planned to take his time in making a decision.

On the campaign trail near Portland, Oregon, the crowds turning out to see Nixon became bitter and hostile. Pat was pushed. Both she and her husband were pelted with pennies. ANYONE WHO MENTIONS $16,000 IS A COMMUNIST! read one sign. Another said, NO MINK COATS FOR NIXON, JUST COLD CASH. Upon seeing that sign Nixon got angry and blurted something out to the crowd that would become one of the most famous lines of his entire career: "There are no mink coats for the Nixons. I'm proud to say my wife, Pat, wears a good old Republican cloth coat."[3]

When Eisenhower finally contacted his beleaguered running mate, it was to say that he was still undecided about what course of action to take. "I don't want to be in the position of condemning an innocent man," he told Nixon on the phone.[4] Eisenhower then suggested that Nixon go on nationwide television and "tell everything you can remember from the day you entered public life." Ike urged Nixon to mention "any money you have ever received." Nixon asked whether Eisenhower would make a decision about his place on the Republican ticket after such a speech. The general remained noncommittal. "Maybe," he said.

Nixon could not hold back his anger. "There comes a

time in matters like this when you've either got to shit or get off the pot," he told Eisenhower. As soon as those words left his mouth Nixon regretted them. He knew he was being disrespectful despite the fact that as a professional soldier, General Eisenhower had heard plenty of cursing and often used swear words himself. For his part, Eisenhower was not offended by Nixon's language, but he was insulted by the younger man's attempt to tell him what to do. That was an offense against his authority and his rank. Eisenhower said nothing for a while, then told Nixon that he would wait a few days after the television speech. As he said good-bye he told Nixon to keep his chin up.

As the political controversy continued to build, the one person who was expected to join in kept quiet. The Democratic presidential nominee, Adlai E. Stevenson, did not join in the attacks on his opponent's running mate. Nonetheless on the day of Richard Nixon's television appearance the newspapers broke a story about Stevenson's having a private fund of money contributed by wealthy supporters too. In defending the fund over the next few days Stevenson was somewhat evasive. The press's failure to go after Stevenson with the same vengeance that they had pursued him enraged Nixon.

Nixon spent the day of September 23 in Los Angeles swimming, reviewing his notes, and thinking. He did not rehearse. On his way to the television studio he appeared calm. When he got to the set he directed the cameraman to stay with him because he did not know whether he would remain seated or get up and walk around the set, which consisted of a desk with a bookcase behind it. Three minutes before he was due to go on the air Nixon panicked. "I just don't think I can go through with this one," he said to Pat.

"Of course you can," she told him. Pat led him to the chair and made sure that he sat down. The light came on and Richard Nixon was on the air.

The speech he gave that night made history in several ways. Richard Nixon's decision to use television to make a political announcement marked the first time a politician had used the new medium to make news. Fifty-eight million people would watch the speech—at that time the largest television audience ever. (Nixon's speech would continue to hold that record until his 1960 presidential debates with John F. Kennedy.) In making broadcast history Nixon also managed to stage an event that was the highlight of his political career. It would remain engraved in people's memories for years.

"My fellow Americans. I come before you tonight as a candidate for the vice presidency . . . and as a man whose honesty and integrity has been questioned," Nixon began. In defending the fund, the assets of which he put at $18,000, Nixon said that since he had not used a penny of that money for himself, it was neither unethical nor immoral. "Every penny of it was used to pay for political expenses that I did not think should be charged to the taxpayers." Furthermore he asserted that none of the contributors had ever received any special compensation.

He said that he and Pat had worked hard and that "every

dime we've got is honestly ours," and he repeated the line about Pat's "good Republican cloth coat," adding, "I always tell her she'd look good in anything." This would be one of Nixon's few public compliments to the woman who devoted her life to him and his political career.

He then spent a couple of minutes talking about Stevenson's private fund and called on the Democrats to make their finances public as well. Then came the historic part of his speech. Nixon said that he expected people would continue to attack him even though he was coming clean. Since he wanted to completely clear his record, Nixon confessed that he had received one gift. "You know what it was? It was a little cocker spaniel in a crate . . . black-and-white spotted. And our little girl—Tricia, the six-year-old—named it Checkers. And you know the kids love that dog and I just want to say this right now, that regardless of what they say about it, we're going to keep it." Nixon's voice faded practically to a squeak when he got to the Checkers part of the speech and he looked as though he were about to break into tears.

In his closing remarks Nixon rose and stood in front of the desk. He said that he knew his audience wondered whether or not he would remain on the Republican ticket. When he said that, even Eisenhower leaned closer to the television set since he, more than anyone, wanted to know the answer. "I don't believe that I ought to quit," Nixon said. "Because I am not a quitter. And, incidentally, Pat is not a quitter. After all, her name is Patricia Ryan, and she was born on St. Patrick's Day (well, almost)—and you know the Irish never quit." After that non sequitur he went on to say that the decision of whether he remained on the ticket was up to Dwight D. Eisenhower. And he urged the audience to let Eisenhower know their opinions by writing and telegraphing the Republican National Committee. As a final jab to the Democrats Nixon said, "Regardless of what happens . . . I am going to campaign up and down America until we drive the crooks and Communists and those that defend them out of Washington."

As soon as he got off the set Nixon said, "I loused it up. I'm sorry." Murray Chotiner and Pat told him he had done a terrific job, but Nixon continued to blame himself. One of the television producers came in to tell him that the studio's telephone switchboard was "lit up like a Christmas tree." Crowds had gathered at Nixon's hotel to cheer him and the hotel's switchboard was overloaded with incoming calls too. One of those calls was from the Hollywood producer Darryl Zanuck who congratulated Richard Nixon on "the most tremendous performance I've ever seen." Overall the audience reaction was mixed. Many people thought that Nixon had been emotionally moving and that he had indeed come clean. Some people were so touched by his speech that they cried. Others believed that he was a phony and that he had created this melodramatic episode about Checkers the dog to play on people's sympathy.

Most important were the telegrams that started pouring in to the Republican National Committee. Three hundred thousand cables and letters signed by more than one million people arrived at Republican headquarters, almost all of them supportive of Nixon. "I like courage," Eisenhower told a crowd in Cleveland soon after Nixon went off the air.

In a cable to Nixon, Eisenhower called the speech "magnificent," but added, "My personal decision is going to be based on personal conclusions." He invited his running mate to meet with him in Wheeling, West Virginia, the following day because, he said, it was obvious that he needed "something more than one single presentation" in order to make up his mind.

Furious at Eisenhower for continuing to hold out, Nixon refused to go to Wheeling. Instead he dictated a letter resigning from the campaign. But Chotiner decided to wait before sending it. In the meantime Nixon continued to insist that he would not go to Wheeling to meet with Eisenhower unless Ike guaranteed his support beforehand. Only after a senior Eisenhower aide tactfully explained that, as the general who had led the Allied forces to victory in Europe, Eisenhower deserved more respect than that did Nixon acquiesce.

No sooner had his plane landed in Wheeling than Eisenhower came aboard to shake Nixon's hand. "General, you didn't need to come out to the airport," Nixon said.

"Why not? You're my boy!" Eisenhower replied. But despite his protestations of support, Ike persisted in questioning Nixon about a rumor that Pat had spent $10,000 to redecorate their home. In fact Eisenhower's staff had investigated the rumor and knew for certain that the frugal Mrs. Nixon sewed all of her home decorations and did not spend that kind of money. But he wanted to make the point that he was Nixon's senior and he was entitled to ask any question he wanted.

At a stadium rally a few hours later Eisenhower finally came out in public for Nixon. "So far as I am concerned, he has not only vindicated himself . . . he stands higher than ever before." Nixon proclaimed that an Eisenhower presidency would be "the cleanest, most honest government America has ever had." Upon leaving the podium Nixon ran into an old friend who told him that his Checkers speech was great. That was the straw that broke the camel's back. After weeks of tension and uncertainty Nixon could no longer hold back his feelings. He put his head on his friend's shoulder and cried.

Even with the Checkers speech behind him, however, Nixon still faced more charges of corruption as the campaign chugged into its final months. In one instance a columnist who claimed to have copies of Nixon's tax returns alleged that he had taken a tax exemption to which he was not entitled. It turned out that these tax returns belonged to another California couple named Richard and Patricia Nixon who were not related to the candidate in any way. The columnist retracted his charges. Then the Democrats produced two letters that allegedly showed that Nixon had accepted more than $52,000 from the oil industry. Nixon called for a full investigation by the Senate Subcommittee on Privileges and Elections and was vindicated when the letters were proved to be forgeries.

Thoroughly embroiled in the combat of this bitter campaign, Nixon enjoyed getting off a few hits of his own, as when he described Stevenson as "a weakling, a waster, and a small-caliber Truman" and the Democrats as being infested with "mobsters, gangsters, and remnants of the old Capone gang." Stevenson countered by calling Nixon "the kind of politician who would cut down a redwood tree, and then mount the stump and make a speech for conservation."

Years later, in his *Memoirs*, Nixon observed that at this point "the taste for politics soured." He was starting to realize that the nasty, combative atmosphere in the political arena was making Pat miserable. He understood that although she would help him however she could, Pat would hate politics for the rest of her life and would always long for a "happy and normal life."

Both sides kept slinging mud all the way to the polls, but it was clear fairly early in the day that Eisenhower and Nixon had won by a large majority. Eisenhower pulled thirty-four million votes, Stevenson twenty-seven million. The Republicans had once again gotten control of the House and the Senate. Despite the sour taste and Pat's personal misery, the political winds of change were definitely blowing in Richard Nixon's direction.

CHAPTER FIVE

Riding This Great Stream of History

AT THE AGE of forty, Richard Nixon was the second-youngest man to hold the office of vice president of the United States. (The youngest was John Breckinridge, who became vice president in 1857 when he was thirty-six years old.) After the election the tension between President Eisenhower and his vice president continued. At the first cabinet meeting of the new administration Nixon said he thought the president was too soft on the Democrats. Patiently Eisenhower explained that although the Republicans, known as the GOP for Grand Old Party, held a majority in both houses of Congress, it was a small majority and the administration would need to cultivate Democrats in order to get its programs through Congress. Despite the friction between them, President Eisenhower asked Vice President Nixon to preside over cabinet and National Security Council meetings. By involving the vice president in NSC affairs President Eisenhower may have done more to upgrade the number-two job than any other president.

As vice president, Richard Nixon continued to build on his role as a hard-hitting anti-Communist campaigner. Sometimes he took his efforts so far that the Eisenhower administration had to cover his tracks, as when Nixon said that American servicemen should be sent to help put down Communist insurgencies in Indochina. Nixon also came out in favor of the infamous McCarthy hearings. The hearings consisted of McCarthy's accusing individuals and organizations of having Communist connections or sympathies. McCarthy was actually taking Nixon's old platform from HUAC and expanding it. But whereas Nixon had made an attempt to look for evidence—even though he twisted it to suit his purposes—McCarthy didn't even bother. His hearings were outright witch hunts, in which anyone whom he branded as even vaguely suspicious was considered guilty without having any opportunity to prove his or her own innocence.

Unlike Nixon, McCarthy appeared to have no political ambitions. He did not care if he offended other members of the Republican party. One indication of this was McCarthy's refusal to vote for confirmation of several Eisenhower appointees. Not only did he refuse to vote along party lines, but McCarthy accused Eisenhower's nominees of having Communist connections and went so far as to obtain a confidential FBI file on one man that alleged the man was a homosexual. His charges served to embarrass the president. Nonetheless Nixon urged President Eisenhower not to criticize the renegade right-wing senator, arguing that it would merely provoke him to become even more flamboyant. He urged instead that they try to cultivate McCarthy and make him part of the team. McCarthy responded by objecting to several of Eisenhower's nominees for cabinet positions, and Nixon's attempts to calm McCarthy down were unsuccessful. After a session that Nixon referred to as "the famous so-called Chicken Lunch," during which he tried to get McCarthy to tone down his attacks, Nixon conceded defeat. "It's probably time we dumped him," he told associates.[1]

But McCarthy's diatribes had already split the Republican party so badly that Adlai Stevenson called it "a political party divided against itself." Not only did McCarthy make wild accusations about Communists in government, he accused the Central Intelligence Agency of being penetrated by Communists. When he tried to subpoena confidential CIA files both Republicans and Democrats became alarmed. While many people were swept along in the wake of Senator McCarthy's disturbing paranoia, President Eisenhower remained skeptical that there were as many Communists loose in the government as McCarthy claimed. Eisenhower dispatched his vice president several times to try again to persuade the conservative senator from Wisconsin to cool down.

Recalling the success of Nixon's Checkers speech, President Eisenhower tapped his vice president to deliver another speech that would rally Americans behind his administration. It was while working on this speech that Nixon had what he considered a great idea. Actually it was more of a portent of things to come. The idea was to "slip a secret recording gadget in the president's office . . . to capture some of those warm, offhand, great-hearted things the Man says, play 'em back, then get them press-released."[2]

On March 13, 1954, Vice President Nixon criticized Senator McCarthy before a television audience of ten million people. During this speech Nixon presented a newly packaged version of Eisenhower proposals that he called the New Look. These proposals included balancing the budget through a 20 percent reduction in defense spending and getting the United States out of its involvement in Korea. (The New Look also contained one of the first public mentions of Vietnam, where American involvement would become one of the most controversial episodes of the coming decade.) McCarthy, in turn, simply commented that he was "sick and tired" of "that prick Nixon" and his "constant yack-yacking."[3]

It was during his first term as vice president that Richard Nixon began to fulfill his lifelong dreams of traveling. All told, Vice President Nixon made nine trips to sixty-one countries. His first trip abroad, in October 1953, included visits to New Zealand, Indonesia, and Vietnam, which was at that time a French colony. The French were just starting to have problems with Vietnamese Communists, who wanted to rid the country of foreign influence and establish a Communist regime. While in Vietnam the vice president donned an army helmet and combat fatigues to witness an artillery battle just north of Hanoi. "We are resolved . . . that you shall not fight unaided," Nixon pledged at an official Vietnamese banquet.

The Korean War, in which American troops had fought Chinese and North Korean Communist forces, had ended in an uneasy cease-fire in July 1953. Nixon's mission in South Korea was to obtain a promise that the South Koreans would refrain from shooting at the North Koreans and accept an armistice negotiated several months earlier. Many South Koreans were not happy about giving up the battle and leaving half of their country under Communist domination.

The threat of Communist insurgency was real in many Asian countries, where impoverished guerrillas were taking up arms to fight landowners and established authorities. The conflict was particularly harsh during Nixon's visit to the Philippines, where one demonstrator held a sign that said GO BACK WARMONGER. Nixon went over and asked the man's name, whereupon the demonstrator backed off. Nixon spoke briefly to the small crowd surrounding the man with the sign and apparently startled them by doing so. Later he said that this encounter showed him that "the only way to deal with Communists is to stand up to them. Otherwise they will exploit your politeness as weakness."[4]

Nixon's first trip to Asia made him aware of the depth and complexity of that continent's problems. It also prepared him well for the presidency because it brought him into contact with heads of state and government officials who would play a continuing role in U.S.–Asia relations through the 1970s.

In 1954, when the French garrison at Dien Bien Phu in Vietnam was assaulted by Vietnamese Communists, Vice President Nixon was one of the first politicians to propose sending American troops to the tiny country. He also proposed a plan called Operation Vulture, which involved using two or three atom bombs in Vietnam to halt the Communist takeover and the fall of French rule there. Vice President Nixon and two other top Republican officials believed that President Eisenhower would implement Operation Vulture when it became clear that the French were doomed.[5] But Eisenhower believed that it would be "completely unconstitutional and indefensible" for him to order a military operation without congressional approval. The United States Constitution gives Congress the power to declare war. Although United States involvement in Korea had not followed such a declaration, and future military actions—including the eventual American participation in Vietnam—were defined more loosely, Eisenhower's position was sound. Nixon then proposed that President Eisenhower send military equipment and technical support to Vietnam, admitting that he was disappointed by the president's refusal to take more decisive action. "I believe that the executive branch of the government has to take the politically unpopular position of facing up to it and doing it, and I personally would support such a decision," Nixon said. But despite his vociferous campaigning, he was unable to persuade President Eisenhower to intervene, and on May 7, 1954, Dien Bien Phu was taken over by the Communists. Several months later the Geneva Accord on Vietnam divided the country into North Vietnam and South Vietnam, and gave the Communists control of the North.

This incident marked the beginning of Richard Nixon's public commitment to fighting communism in Southeast Asia, and it was also the first time that he took a strong public stand on a foreign policy issue. He was the only member of the Eisenhower administration to take that politically unpopular stand. Although there was no hope of his getting his ideas put into action at that point, Vice President Nixon drew up a proposed program aimed at training Vietnamese troops to fight against the Communists. The United States would provide naval backup and air power, sending in its own troops only if necessary. Above all, the United States would refuse to enter into any talks with the Communists and would never, ever surrender to them. Although not enacted by the Eisenhower administration, this program would eventually become part of the cornerstone of Nixon's own Vietnam policy when he became president fourteen years later.

When he wasn't traveling around the world Vice President Nixon was often traveling around the country campaigning for local Republicans. In fact he did so much traveling that he soon became known as a "one-man GOP task force." He continued his hard-hitting anti-Communist line, at one point going so far as to say that President Eisenhower had discovered "a blueprint for socializing America" that contained the Democrats' plans for socializing medicine, housing, and agriculture. Nixon claimed that this plan, which Eisenhower had uncovered shortly after coming to office, would have created a $40 billion national debt. However, the plan had never existed, as reporters who tried to get hold of the document found out. Nixon's campaign manager, Murray Chotiner, defended the use of the term "socialist blueprint" by saying that it was a metaphor for, or a figurative description of, the Democrats' intentions. In fact no copy of any such blueprint was ever found.

During his travels Vice President Nixon was shrewd at building up a wide political base among the rank-and-file members of his own party, but he never mastered the niceties of diplomatic and social functions, which he described as "extremely boring." And although his acting talents stood him in good stead in front of an audience, Nixon found it nearly impossible to disguise his boredom at parties. A Republican party leader said that Nixon "ached for people to like him" but did not know how to make friends. People regarded him as a little cold and standoffish. "No one would look forward to spending a week with Nixon fishing," the Republican leader said. One

Washington socialite said that when Vice President Nixon arrived at a party "it was as if the high school monitor had suddenly appeared," and went on to describe both Nixons as "wooden and stiff." Pat was generally seen as the more gracious of the two. One reporter wrote that Pat always had "the right reply, the right greeting, the gracious smile." She had learned "to be the silent, demure partner of the great man who is only a heartbeat away from the White House." But although the press was kind to Pat, it did not treat Richard Nixon as nicely. Some cartoonists portrayed him as living in a sewer. Pat canceled the family subscription to the *Washington Post* because she worried that her daughters would get upset at seeing their father caricatured in the editorial cartoons. "We don't have as many good times as we used to,"[6] Pat said, as she began yet another campaign to get her husband to promise he would retire from politics when his first term as vice president was over. She insisted that Tricia and Julie needed to have a stable home life and that this could be better accomplished if Nixon went back to Whittier, California, and resumed his law practice.

Although Nixon enjoyed the competitive aspect of politics, signs of stress were taking their toll and he had started seeing a New York medical doctor for his insomnia. Although the doctor was an internist, not a psychiatrist, many people have speculated that Nixon was undergoing Freudian analysis.[7] However, neither the doctor nor Nixon has ever revealed the confidential nature of his treatment. Perhaps as a result of the ongoing tension, and possibly because of Pat's persuasiveness, Richard Nixon did promise that he would get out of politics and not seek reelection in 1956. He even signed a statement for Pat to that effect, but instead of giving it to her for safekeeping he held on to it himself.

On September 24, 1955, Richard Nixon was reading the newspaper when he received a phone call that changed his life. "The President has had a coronary," announced Jim Hagerty, one of Eisenhower's aides.

Nixon sat there silently for several minutes before asking, "Are they sure? I don't think we should announce it as a heart attack until we are absolutely sure."[8]

The diagnosis was certain, Nixon was told.

In his *Memoirs*, Nixon described how he sat in his living room in a state of shock, while thoughts raced through his mind. "It was like a great physical weight holding me down in the chair," he observed. Realizing that he was now in the delicate position of heading the nation without appearing to take over entirely, Nixon pondered a course of action. He decided to play it cool and to do as little as possible so as not to be accused of seeming too eager to handle the reins of power.

In the meantime Congress and the cabinet were thrown into a crisis. Although the Constitution provides for the vice president to become president "in case of the removal of the president from office, or of his death, resignation, or inability to discharge the powers and duties of said office," it offers no guidelines on what to do if the president is disabled. What if he was able to function mentally but was unable to sign his name, as might be the case after a stroke? What if the president only recovered partially? Which branch of the government had the right to assess his condition and decide that the vice president would have to take over?

No sooner had news of the president's heart attack hit the press than the newspapers started speculating on Nixon's chances of being nominated as the Republican candidate for president in 1956. They simply assumed that Eisenhower, should he survive his heart attack, would not run for reelection. Professional politicians within the Republican party began to back Richard Nixon. However, Eisenhower's chief of staff, Sherman Adams, resented that power shift to Vice President Nixon and the resentment sparked a power struggle even as Eisenhower lay in the hospital. Although Nixon was quick to remind the cabinet that this was still an Eisenhower administration, his critics said that he moved to take charge with more speed and audacity than the situation required. The two weeks that Vice President Nixon took the helm for Eisenhower were basically uneventful, but Nixon described himself as "drained" during that "period of indecision." Foremost in his mind was the terrifying question of nuclear war. In the unlikely event of an attack, would it be his responsibility to launch nuclear weapons in retaliation?

Two weeks after his heart attack Eisenhower summoned his vice president to the hospital in Denver where he was being treated and thanked Nixon for all that he had done. But although he called Nixon "a darn good young man,"

Eisenhower was quietly worried that people would start to think of Nixon as presidential material. Even though the press had decided that Eisenhower was not going to run for reelection, the president had enough spunk to want to get back into the race. He was simply waiting for his doctors to give him the okay. The last thing he wanted was an ambitious, frisky young vice president snapping at his heels. So Eisenhower began sending out mixed signals about Nixon, praising him and subtly undermining him at the same time. "The country still considers him a bit immature," Eisenhower commented.[9]

Nixon was hurt by this. He admired President Eisenhower and wanted the chief to like him. (Although Eisenhower had thanked him briefly in the hospital and wrote him a thank-you note a few days later, Nixon would later note in his *Memoirs* that the president thanked him for his efforts only three times during the eight years they served together.) But if Eisenhower's indifference was disappointing to Nixon, we can only imagine how he felt when Eisenhower decided to continue running for reelection and told Nixon that it would be better if he took a cabinet post instead of running for reelection as vice president. Eisenhower insisted that it would be better for the country as well as for Nixon if he acquired more day-to-day administrative experience. But what he really wanted was to get rid of Nixon, whom he regarded as a political threat. He told Nixon that if he stayed on as vice president, people would always consider him an understudy, but if he accepted a cabinet post he would be seen as "a halfback in his own right." Eisenhower's gambit took a heavy toll on Nixon—physically, mentally, and emotionally. He wanted to do the right thing by his party, but he also wanted desperately to remain in the running. He came to see Eisenhower less as someone to be admired and more as a man who was "more complex and devious than most people realized."[10]

The movement to "dump Nixon" from the reelection ticket grew within the Republican party. Some politicians were suspicious of Nixon's continual campaigning. Others believed that he had no platform other than his own personal ambition, and charged that he used his anti-Communist ideology only to further his career. Some referred to Nixon as a man "of artifice and intuition," meaning that Nixon sensed intuitively what people needed to hear and that he would manufacture his comments in order to manipulate the response.

Keeping in mind his promise to Pat, Nixon reconsidered an offer to head a law firm in California, and on March 8, 1956, he drafted a letter saying that he would not seek reelection. But before handing it in he thought some more. Since Eisenhower had a heart condition, and since he, Nixon, had experience in standing in for the president during an emergency, he had a personal responsibility to the country, he reasoned, to stay on the ticket as vice president. But the "dump Nixon" movement had spread through the Republican party, and it took several months of heated campaigning for Nixon to emerge as the victor. Eisenhower held off from endorsing him until the last minute, when in August 1956 Richard Nixon was officially renominated for vice president at the Republican convention in San Francisco.

So much for his promise that he would get out of politics. Even though he had been aware, ever since the Checkers speech, of how uncomfortable Pat was with their life-style, Richard Nixon was hooked. "Once you are riding this great stream of history you can't get out," he said years later.[11]

CHAPTER SIX

You Won't Have Richard Nixon to Kick Around Anymore

AT THE OUTSET of the 1956 campaign President Eisenhower offered Vice President Nixon a few words of advice: Tone down your anticommunism, don't attack the Democrats so harshly, and don't claim that the Eisenhower–Nixon team is perfect. In 1948 Harry Truman had battled his way through to victory with the campaign cry of "Give 'em hell!" Eisenhower urged Nixon to "Give 'em heaven."

Of course, heaven is not an appropriate way to describe any political campaign, even though this one was considerably gentler than the campaign of 1952. Nixon's proximity to the nation's highest office was now an issue, calling into question his character and his ability to hold that office in the event of another presidential heart attack. President Eisenhower insisted that he was in excellent health and praised Richard Nixon. "There is no man in the history of America who has had such a careful preparation as has Vice President Nixon for carrying out the duties of the presidency, if that should ever fall on him."[1]

Since the last election Nixon's campaign team had swelled from a staff of two advisers plus secretaries to a considerably larger contingent. Much to Nixon's dismay, his campaign manager, Murray Chotiner, had been hauled before a Senate committee. Chotiner, whose mudslinging tactics had angered many people, had allegedly used his connections with Vice President Nixon in order to benefit his legal practice. Chotiner had received large amounts of money from manufacturers who supplied uniforms to the United States Army. He had also been charged with representing two hundred Las Vegas bookies and gamblers. The Chotiner investigation had started during the period when Eisenhower was trying to persuade Nixon to get off the Republican ticket and accept a cabinet job. Although Nixon had praised Chotiner as a good man who had been completely honest during his years as Nixon's campaign manager, he had told Eisenhower that if anything did turn up on Chotiner, "the administration has no relationship at all."[2] Although Chotiner refused to testify and the Senate committee dropped the case, Nixon prudently cut his ties with Chotiner for the 1956 campaign and put together a new team. One of the men who came aboard was H. R. Haldeman, an account executive for the advertising company J. Walter Thompson. Haldeman took a paid leave of absence from his job to work as a full-time volunteer for the vice president's reelection. Herb Klein, a young reporter for the *San Diego Union,* also took a leave of absence to work as assistant press secretary during the campaign. Nixon's faithful secretary, Rose Mary Woods, helped to manage the staff, coordinate schedules, and perform executive secretarial functions. Nixon had several speech writers working for him even though he usually liked to prepare his own speeches. He was obsessive about drawing up outlines and revising his text over and over again. Herb Klein said that the men working for him gave him ideas "but it all goes through that meat grinder of a mind he's got."

With a subtler tone than the one he used to win the vice presidency in 1952, Nixon went around the country saying that the Republicans were bringing America "peace, prosperity, and progress." The press corps following him got so tired of hearing him repeat himself that they made up names for his standard lines. When he talked about "peace and prosperity to boot," they called it "the old shoe" speech. And when he said that "every man can hold up Dwight Eisenhower to his children as a man who has faith in God, faith in America," they called it Nixon's "weight-lifting act." He did speak out for racial equality during the campaign, even though that earned him the enmity of segregationists. All in all, he ran such an organized campaign that NBC news correspondent David Brinkley called it "the best operation I've ever seen," adding that "when it comes to politics I am hard to impress."

If he got *A*s with Brinkley for organization, Nixon barely passed with many other members of the press corps who were skeptical that this was really "a new Nixon." But whereas Nixon previously slashed and burned a swath of accusations against his opponents, this time he hardly raised an eyebrow, even when the Democratic presidential candidate, Adlai Stevenson, called him "a man of many masks." Stevenson said that the American public did not want candidates "who have to be changed" and that he doubted that Richard Nixon had truly metamorphosed into the "Little Lord Fauntleroy of the Republican party." Stevenson talked about "Nixonland," a place where poison-pen letters, anonymous phone calls, and lies were everyday occurrences. But Nixon did not take the bait, commenting only that he did not want to be known as "a political Jack the Ripper."

Although he found it frustrating to campaign with one arm tied behind his back, Nixon found that it paid off. He and Eisenhower won reelection by a stunning margin: thirty-five million to Stevenson's twenty-five million. But the Republicans failed to regain control of Congress, and many Republicans blamed Nixon for not being tough enough on the Democrats during the campaign.

While it could not really be called a high point, certainly the most memorable event of Vice President Nixon's second term was his 1958 trip to South America. The trip started in Montevideo, Uruguay, where he and Pat were greeted by chanting crowds. Despite the concerns of his Secret Service agents, Nixon often stopped the car and got out to work the crowd. Pat visited orphanages and children's hospitals, shaking as many as one thousand hands in one day. In Argentina Nixon went so far as to skip an official reception so that he could join a workers' rally and meet the working people. "Free labor and dictatorship are completely incompatible," he told them.

While Uruguay and Argentina had predominantly middle-class populations, other South American countries, such as Peru and Venezuela, had populations that were largely poor. Most of those nations' wealth was concentrated in the hands of a few. Many of those who suffered from inequality were attracted to Marxist philosophy, which preaches that every person shall be compensated according to his needs. To these people the United States represented the evils of capitalism. And the communism that Nixon found so abhorrent held some appeal.

The mood of the journey turned angry in Lima, Peru, where demonstrators held up signs saying FUERA NIXON, or "Nixon Go Home." A few protestors went further, carrying placards that said MUERA NIXON, or "Death to Nixon." Having decided, as in the past, that the best approach was direct confrontation, Nixon left the safety of his car to face the protestors outside a Lima university. As he walked into the middle of the crowd some of the demonstrators cheered *"El gringo tiene cojones!"* meaning "The Yankee has balls." But others were enraged by his daring and began to throw oranges, bottles, and rocks at him.

"Let's get out of here," Nixon said to his aides, one of whom had just received a broken tooth when a rock had struck his mouth. When Nixon reached his car he stood up in the backseat and shouted, "You are the worst kind of cowards!" Arriving back at his hotel in downtown Lima, Nixon found that a new, angrier group of protestors were massed in the plaza outside. This time when Nixon got out of his car to walk through the mob he was not only pelted with rocks and fruit, but spit upon. As he got to the door of his hotel a demonstrator with a mouth full of chewed tobacco spit a grisly gob in the vice president's face. Nixon fought to control his temper, but later said that "spitting in a person's face is the most infuriating insult ever conceived by man." Just before he walked inside he kicked the demonstrator in the shin. "I've never been more proud of him," said Pat Nixon, who had been watching the melee from an upstairs window.

After a brief stop in Quito, Ecuador, where Nixon strolled into a local barbershop for an impromptu haircut, and an uneventful stopover in Bogotá, Colombia, the vice-presidential entourage headed for Caracas, Venezuela. There the Communist party had organized massive anti-Nixon demonstrations and the left-wing press had fed Venezuelans' growing anti-American antagonism with editorial cartoons of "Tricky Dick" showing Nixon with fangs. Having been warned in advance that the mood in Caracas would be ugly, Nixon considered backing off. But that was not his style. By the time the plane taxied to a landing at Caracas's airport, thousands of people had gathered to jeer him. "They aren't friendly, Mr. Vice President," an aide whispered as Nixon peered out the airplane door. Nonetheless he and Pat made their way along a red carpet lined with soldiers standing at attention while the mob screamed obscenities and threw rocks and fruit at them. As they got to the end of the honor guard, a little girl came out to give flowers to Pat Nixon. Pat leaned down and hugged her. As the band started to play the national anthem of Venezuela, the crowd started spitting at the Nixons. So much gob and goo rained down on them that it ran down Pat's face and her outfit was ruined. But both of them remained standing at attention throughout the national anthem.

Accompanying Nixon to the hotel, the Venezuelan foreign minister tried to wipe some spit off Nixon's suit, but Nixon said he planned to burn the clothes as soon as possible and refused to accept the foreign minister's apology for the crowd's behavior. "If your government doesn't have the guts and good sense to control a mob like the one at the airport, there soon will be no freedom for anyone in Venezuela," he hissed, adding that the crowd was organized by Communists. No sooner had he spoken than they drove into a massive roadblock. This time the stones that were thrown at them were large, heavy rocks. As the rocks hit the car, people mobbed it from the side streets but the driver managed to escape. Weaving through another side street came a second mob of about two hundred people. They swarmed all over the car, smashing the windows with rocks, beer cans, and pieces of pipe. A piece of broken glass struck the foreign minister in the eye. In the car behind the vice president's, Pat Nixon sat calmly while her vehicle was pelted with stones. She was worried that her husband's car would be overturned or that he would be dragged into the crowd. When they managed to get away from this mob, Nixon ordered the motorcade to head for the United States Embassy instead of going through with his scheduled stop at the tomb of South American liberator Simón Bolívar.

At an afternoon news conference Nixon's tone was both conciliatory and angry. While he believed that the mob did not represent the people of Venezuela, he said, "It's certainly not pleasant to go through a shower of spit and have a man spit directly in the face of my wife." And he blamed the Communists for creating that chaos. The reporters gave him a standing ovation when he was finished.

Meanwhile news that the vice president was under attack had reached Washington and President Eisenhower dispatched two companies of the 101st Airborne Division to Puerto Rico. He also put two companies of marines on alert at the American base in Guantanamo in the Caribbean, calling his emergency military plan Operation Poor Richard. When "Poor Richard" heard about it, he was disturbed. Caracas had quieted down but now the Venezuelan press was reporting that the United States was preparing an invasion. Nixon made a public statement that the United States was shifting troops from one American base to another and that there was no need for concern.

Praised by many for his coolheadedness while under attack, Richard Nixon was philosophical after his return to the

United States. Remaining calm during a crisis was not hard, he said. "The difficult task is . . . after it is all over. I get a real letdown after one of these issues," he confided.[3]

Several months after returning from Venezuela Vice President Nixon got another chance to stand up against Communists. That historic trip brought him to Moscow, where he met with Soviet premier Nikita Khrushchev. Before leaving Washington, Nixon was advised by President Eisenhower to keep "a cordial, almost light atmosphere." But as one might have expected, sparks flew as the feisty anti-Communist campaigner locked horns with the equally feisty anticapitalist Soviet leader. While the two men stood in a model kitchen that was being built as part of an American exhibition intended to show Russians how Americans lived, Khrushchev said that Soviet progress would surpass American achievements in a few years. "You don't know everything," Nixon countered.

"If I don't know everything, you don't know anything about communism except fear of it," Khrushchev replied, going on to condemn the United States for producing too many different kinds of appliances. Nixon switched the subject, saying that it was preferable to compete in appliance production rather than rockets. Khrushchev took that remark as a threat and the argument escalated as the two men started poking each other to emphasize their points. Later this confrontation became known as the "kitchen debate."

Both the Venezuela and Moscow confrontations paid off for Nixon politically at home. His popularity shot up and he easily won the Republican presidential nomination in 1960. By this time his daughter Tricia was fourteen and Julie was twelve. They had become accustomed to their parents' traveling before, during, and after campaigns. Pat and Richard Nixon had never allowed their daughters to be interviewed during any of Nixon's campaigns. Pat insisted on bringing them up with affection and strict regard for the value of money. Although many of their friends got one dollar a week for allowance, Tricia and Julie got fifty cents each. And although as vice president their father earned $35,000 a year with an additional $10,000 thrown in for expenses, Tricia and Julie helped their mother with the housework and watched as she ironed their father's shirts, darned his socks, and sewed up any small rips or tears in his clothing. Both of them adored their father, whose idea of relaxing was to spend an evening at home playing with Checkers, their four cats, and his two girls. On those rare occasions that he came home for dinner, they set the table with the best china, candlesticks, and flowers. Tricia shared her father's love of baseball and enjoyed going with him to watch the Washington Senators play. But in temperament she was more like her mother, quiet and reserved. Julie was talkative and outgoing. Even people who did not care for Richard Nixon's politics or personality conceded that he had a wonderful family. And as he prepared to take on Massachusetts senator John F. Kennedy in the 1960 presidential race, his wife and daughters put their personal dislike of politics aside to support him in as many ways as they could.

The 1960 run for the White House marked a turning point in American politics. It would become the first national political race to be organized with television coverage as a focal priority. So far in his career, Richard Nixon had been cannily able to use television to his advantage. But that had been for individual speeches, such as the Checkers speech. This time he needed a strategy that would draw television coverage of such events as whistle-stop campaigning and impromptu news conferences as well as formal campaign speeches. One of his supporters pointed out the need for him to "always project as the relaxed, confident, fresh, and unwearied candidate," urging that he make sure that he get enough sleep in order to avoid fatigue. For the first time a candidate's physical appearance as seen on television would have as much impact on the voters as his message.

Nixon agreed with that advice in principle, but he was too hard-driving and relentless a campaigner to be able to take it to heart. Basically Nixon found it difficult to take advice from anyone, even his closest supporters and aides. Just as he had been a loner when surrounded by loving family and a close community during his childhood, he was a loner even when surrounded by people who admired him and who were devoted to helping him win. (His secretary, Rose Mary Woods, was so loyal that she once poured a drink on a man's head after he insulted her boss.) President Eisenhower urged Nixon not to go on television to debate John F. Kennedy as Kennedy had proposed. Eisenhower advised that since Nixon was already a nationally recognized figure and Kennedy was not, the debates would give Kennedy needed recognition while Nixon would gain nothing. President Eisenhower also doubted the value of debates, believing that they were theatrical rather than substantive. Viewers would respond to the candidate with the quickest, wittiest response rather than to his position on a particular issue.

But Nixon had loved debating ever since high school and had recently honed his skills in Moscow with no less an opponent than the preeminent leader of the Communist world. He had nothing to fear from a young senator and decided to take on the challenge. President Eisenhower offered to help by sending his own media adviser, a former television producer. But Nixon again said no. Eisenhower took this as a sign of disrespect and from that point on proceeded to undermine Nixon's candidacy. At one famous press conference a reporter for *Time* magazine said, "Nixon almost wants to claim that he has had a great deal of practice at being president," and asked if Eisenhower could come up with one idea of Nixon's that he had used. "If you give me a week, I might think of one," Eisenhower answered.[4] No sooner had he made that remark than he phoned Nixon to apologize. But behind his back Eisenhower still resented Nixon for not accepting a cabinet post in 1956. Had he done so, Eisenhower grumbled, Nixon would be in a stronger position to campaign for the presidency.

The first debate, held in Chicago, aired on September 26, 1960. An unprecedented eighty million viewers tuned in. Nixon, who had been nursing an injured knee, banged it on a door going into the studio. His face turned pale. The fatigue of campaigning had also taken its toll, and it showed. He had lost so much weight that his neck looked scrawny and his shirt collar stuck out around it. Nixon also refused to wear heavy television makeup, using only a face powder called Lazy Shave to cover his heavy beard. By contrast Kennedy was relaxed, having spent the previous week getting a suntan. Theodore H. White, the author of *The Making of the President, 1960,* described the extreme contrast between the two men. Nixon looked "tense, almost frightened . . . haggard-looking to the point of sickness." He appeared to slouch and when his Lazy Shave powder became sweaty, his eyes looked like "exaggerated hollows of blackness, his jaws, jowls, and face drooping with strain."[5] His heavy beard looked even darker on television, giving him an unkempt, vaguely sinister appearance. Having banged his knee, Nixon found it painful to stand at the podium throughout the debate and this, too, contributed to the discomfort on his face. He looked so grim that his mother called up after the show to ask if he was feeling all right. Nixon's physical appearance on television gave many viewers the impression that he was cold, heartless, and insincere. His physical discomfort on the set translated into shiftiness and evasion. Put simply, Nixon did not come across as a man to be trusted. Kennedy, on the other hand, looked as poised and confident as a captain at the helm.

The debate was really no more than a news conference, with the candidates fielding questions from reporters on issues such as foreign and domestic policy, as well as

Nixon's favorite topic, international communism. Although there was nothing particularly dramatic about either candidate's approach, the outcome of the debate was astonishing. While the press and the television audience agreed that Kennedy had won the debate, most of the people who listened to the debate on the radio believed that Nixon had won. In other words, Nixon had spoken clearly and with substance. But his appearance was so disturbing that hardly anyone watching him was able to focus on the content of his message. Nixon had, in effect, lost the election that night.

The second debate, held in Washington, D.C., aired on October 7, 1960. This time Nixon allowed himself to be fully made up for the camera. In order to prevent Nixon from sweating, his assistants made sure that the air conditioners were turned up high. The lighting appeared to favor Nixon this time too, but when Kennedy arrived he complained about lighting conditions and the temperature in the studio. Both were readjusted to his specifications. Once on the air the second debate was more confrontational than the first, with Nixon attacking Kennedy for criticizing the Eisenhower administration instead of Premier Khrushchev. "At the present time, Communist prestige in the world is at an all-time low and American prestige is at an all-time high," Nixon declared. Kennedy countered by claiming that he was as tough on defending the country from communism as was Nixon. "I'm talking about our willingness to bear any burdens in order to maintain our own freedom," he said, claiming that the Democrats would give Americans better defense as well as better social services without raising taxes. Nixon said that the Republicans cared about social welfare and progress as much as the Democrats did and said that the Republicans would "move America forward faster." He also appealed to the audience to give him credit for being as sincere as Kennedy. This time both the press and the television audience believed that Nixon had gained the advantage over Kennedy.

On October 13, 1960, Nixon was in Hollywood, Kennedy in New York City. The third debate was transmitted by satellite. A few days before the debate, Kennedy had accused Nixon of being "trigger-happy" over the defense of two tiny nationalist Chinese islands, Quemoy and Matsu, which were being bombed by Communist Chinese forces. During the debate Nixon answered that charge by asking Kennedy to name one Republican president that led the United States into a war. "There were three Democratic presidents who led us into war. I do not mean by that that one party is a war party and the other party is a peace party. But I do say that any statement to the effect that the Republican party is trigger-happy is belied by the record," he said. Some observers gave Nixon a slight edge in this final debate. Although the first debate gave Kennedy a clear edge, the two candidates were running neck and neck in the polls as the campaign entered its final twenty-five days.

Nixon headed toward the conclusion of his campaign with as many references as possible to his experience as vice president. During his term, Nixon pointed out, he had attended 163 cabinet meetings and 217 meetings of the National Security Council. He had visited fifty-four countries and had conferred with thirty-five presidents, nine prime ministers, two emperors, and the Shah of Iran. He claimed to have met 173 times with President Eisenhower, and commented, "I have sat with the president as he made these lonely decisions." The possibility that Eisenhower was "lonely" because Nixon had nothing to contribute was not lost on his critics, one of whom quipped that Richard Nixon was skilled in "leadership by association."[6]

If people were skeptical of Vice President Nixon's abilities, they were altogether charmed by Pat Nixon's down-to-earth manner and warmth. Even though she hated campaigning, Pat traveled thousands of miles to help her husband, speaking to women's groups and visiting children's hospitals with seemingly limitless energy. On the other hand, this dedicated drive struck her critics as an excessive attempt to be superhuman and they nicknamed her "Plastic Pat." But unlike her husband, Pat Nixon genuinely enjoyed meeting people and expressed real concern for those in need. She loved to travel and was constantly curious about new people and places. Most important, Pat was able to be moved emotionally by those with whom she came in contact.

Since John F. Kennedy's wife, Jackie, was pregnant at the time, she did not travel very much during the 1960 campaign. A glamorous socialite, Jackie was both admired and detested for her Parisian designer clothes and her expensive tastes. After hearing a rumor that she spent $30,000 a year on clothes, Jackie quipped, "I couldn't spend that much unless I wore sable underwear." Pat

Nixon, on the other hand, wore ready-to-wear, off-the-rack garments that were low-key and tasteful. She struck an amicable chord with middle-class and working-class Americans, who found her gracious without being threatening. The two candidates behaved very differently toward their wives in public. Kennedy held Jackie's hand and appeared affectionate, whereas Nixon avoided touching Pat altogether and often ignored her at public functions. But in fact Nixon was completely loyal to Pat, whereas Kennedy's extramarital affairs were common knowledge among Washington insiders.[7]

Beyond their clear differences there were some startling similarities between the two candidates. To start with, both were young to be seeking the nation's highest office. Nixon was forty-seven and Kennedy forty-three. Both of them had older brothers who had died. Both of them had been junior officers in the navy. At the time of the 1960 campaign Nixon was better known than Kennedy because he had been vice president for eight years and because of his exposure during the Alger Hiss case. Both men were politically savvy, very intelligent, and highly ambitious. But Nixon took himself and his ambition with utter seriousness, whereas Kennedy had a sense of humor about himself. "Do you realize the responsibility I have?" he joked. "I'm the only person between Nixon and the White House." Although the two candidates had many similar characteristics, the public preferred Kennedy's camera-ready charm to Nixon's seriousness.

As the two candidates battled their way through the final weeks of the campaign, Nixon's temper grew shorter. One afternoon, when some Kennedy supporters heckled him at a rally in Michigan, Nixon snapped, "I have been heckled by experts. So don't try anything on me or we'll take care of you."

Two weeks before election day former president Harry Truman came out strongly against Nixon, who, Truman said, would probably soon be retiring from politics. Truman suggested that when he did so Nixon could open an amusement park called "Nixonland" where he could put to work "his considerable gifts of showmanship and his ability to create all kinds of illusions."

Nixon wrapped up the last two days of his campaign attending rallies in Anchorage, Alaska; Madison, Wisconsin; Detroit, Michigan; Chicago, Illinois; and finally Los Angeles, California. That burst of energy seemed to put Nixon in the lead on election day and some political analysts believe that if he had had another few days to continue at that pace, he might have turned the tide. The race was too close to call on election day.

As the returns started filtering in from the East Coast around 5:00 P.M. Pacific time on November 8, Richard Nixon, in California, was dismayed to find himself running even with Kennedy. By 11:00 P.M. Nixon was sure that he would not win, although he was equally sure that those who were forecasting a landslide victory for Kennedy were also wrong. Just before midnight Pat, Tricia, and Julie stopped by his suite. "Hi, Daddy. How's the election going?" asked Tricia. Nixon told her he believed he was losing and Tricia started to cry, explaining, "I'm not crying because of myself, but for you and Mommy. You have worked so hard and so long."[8] Nixon wanted to concede the election at that point but Pat refused to allow it, saying that too many people had devoted themselves to the Nixon campaign for him to give in so easily. She suggested that he go downstairs to thank them instead of conceding. He did so, ending his speech by acknowledging that if John F. Kennedy won the election, he would have Richard Nixon's full support.

At 4:00 A.M. Nixon fell asleep. When he woke up at 6:00 A.M. he learned that he had won twenty-six states and Kennedy twenty-three. Nixon had won 49.6 percent of the popular vote. But he had lost the election because the states Kennedy had won accounted for more electoral votes. Kennedy had 303 electoral votes, while Nixon had 219. It was the closest popular vote in American history. Victory could have been Richard Nixon's had just a few thousand people voted differently.

In the aftermath of the election there were accusations that fraudulent electoral practices had taken place in Texas and Illinois. Nixon's family wanted him to demand a recount, or at least an investigation, but Nixon did not want to follow that advice. "I could think of no worse example for nations abroad," he said, than for governments that were trying to put free electoral procedures into effect for the first time to see "the United States wrangling over the results of our presidential election."[9] Even worse, to Nixon, would have been the suggestion that "the presidency itself could be stolen by thievery at the ballot box."

The morning after election day Julie Nixon asked her

father what he was going to do. He announced that they would move their home base from Washington to California, where he would go back to practicing law. Pat hoped that his retirement from politics would allow him more time to spend with his family, and for a while, at least, that was true. After so many years of public life, Nixon at last had time to go swimming with his daughters and to really get to know them. He had been out of touch with their growth and, apparently, with the changing times, because he expressed dismay when he found out that fourteen-year-old Tricia was starting to get interested in boys. "Isn't she too young?" he asked Pat.

"Dick, you've got a lot to learn," she answered.

In 1961 Nixon decided to write an autobiographical account of his political career. Called *Six Crises*, it covered the Hiss case, the Checkers speech, President Eisenhower's heart attack, the Caracas violence, his "kitchen debate" with Khrushchev, and his unsuccessful bid to win the presidency in 1960. After a few months of working on it he declared that writing the book was "crisis number seven." President John F. Kennedy, who had won a Pulitzer Prize for his book *Profiles in Courage*, encouraged Nixon to work on it. (In fact Kennedy's book had been ghost written while Nixon wrote his book himself.) In *Six Crises* he explained how he arrived at key decisions and analyzed his own mood swings before, during, and after each "exquisite agony" of crisis. Nixon also revealed that he enjoyed the high energy peaks of each incident. Published in 1962, the book became a best-seller and brought Richard Nixon more than $200,000 in royalties. Years later he urged his White House staff to read it again. "A hell of a book . . . everything you need to know is in it," he said. H. R. Haldeman, the man who had worked with Nixon during his second vice-presidential campaign and would eventually become President Nixon's chief of staff, worked closely with Nixon during the research phase of *Six Crises*.

When Nixon decided to run for governor of California in 1962, Haldeman, who had also been an aide in the 1960 presidential elections, became his campaign manager, bringing with him his friend John Ehrlichman, a real estate lawyer from Seattle. Nixon's secretary, Rose Mary Woods, also continued to work for him.

Nixon's campaign for the presidency had been direct and statesmanlike, but his campaign for the governorship was a throwback to his earlier political tactics. Murray Chotiner reemerged as a force behind the campaign, advising Haldeman from behind the scenes. Haldeman engineered a pamphlet from a phony group called "Committee for the Preservation of the Democratic Party." Sent to registered Democrats, the pamphlet charged that Governor Pat Brown was under the control of left-wing extremists who were out to destroy the Democratic party. It also contained a photograph that had been altered to show Brown bowing to Soviet leader Khrushchev. Nixon approved the pamphlet. Later both he and Haldeman denied that they had intended to do anything illegal such as falsifying a photograph. They also distributed bumper stickers that asked IS BROWN PINK?

Brown's campaign countered with a leaflet distributed by another phony group called "Independent Voters of California." It contained a copy of the deed to Nixon's home in Washington. Highlighted was a clause that prevented Nixon from selling the home to a black or a Jew. Nixon had signed the agreement. John Ehrlichman advised Nixon to say that he had signed the document without reading it carefully but Nixon chose not to respond, believing that most of his supporters would have approved of such a discriminatory clause themselves. Pat Nixon, who had kept her promise not to make any speeches, began to speak out. "These smears are hard on our family and particularly on our teenage daughters," she said, adding, "Dick has always attempted to carry on his campaign on a high plane."[10]

Amid the innuendo Nixon attempted to put forth a platform for higher teachers' salaries, more freeways, better water, a larger police force, budget reduction, and anti-Communist programs in the schools. But the race remained a campaign of personalities. Meanwhile the Democrats pounded the pavement to get people registered by election time. On election day Nixon monitored the returns. By midnight he knew the verdict. Actually Nixon lost the governorship by fewer than 300,000 votes. "Losing California after losing the Presidency—well, it's like being bitten by a mosquito after being bitten by a rattlesnake," he said.[11]

Richard Nixon had stayed awake sitting alone throughout the night, and by 8:00 A.M. he was tense and exhausted. He told Herb Klein, his press secretary, that he would not face the press after his defeat. "Damn it, I am not going to do it," he blurted out. Then he went to thank his staff, many of whom were crying. As Nixon looked up at a television set he saw that Herb Klein was facing an angry group of reporters. "Where's Nixon?" they jeered.

There are several versions of what happened next. According to one, Nixon did an about-face, announcing, "I'm going down there." According to another version, Haldeman became enraged when he heard the reporters jeering. He blamed the "liberal press" for Nixon's defeat and said, "They should be told just where the hell to get off." No matter which version is correct, the next few minutes became Nixonian history.

Richard Nixon stalked into the press room and announced, "Now that Mr. Klein has made a statement, now that all the members of the press are so delighted that I lost, I would just like to make a statement of my own." At first he thanked the press for their coverage and said that he believed in a free press. But his mood became surly as he continued. "For sixteen years, ever since the Hiss case, you've had a lot of fun—a lot of fun—that you've had an opportunity to attack me and I think I've given as good as I've taken. . . . I leave you gentlemen now and you will now write it. You will interpret it. That's your right. But as I leave you I want you to know—just think how much you're going to be missing. You won't have Richard Nixon to kick around anymore because, gentlemen, this is my last press conference."

PART II

CHAPTER SEVEN

The New Nixon

ALTHOUGH RICHARD NIXON was angry at losing the California governorship, he was smart enough to realize that maybe the loss was not so bad. He could have found himself stalled politically at the level of state governor when what he really wanted was to challenge President Kennedy again in 1964.[1]

But President Kennedy was assassinated on November 22, 1963, in Dallas, Texas. For millions of Americans his murder symbolized a loss of faith in the innate goodness of American society. Kennedy was seen by many as the embodiment of the ideals set forth in his inaugural speech when he said, "Ask not what your country can do for you. Rather ask what you can do for your country." The Kennedy administration negotiated the first nuclear test ban treaty with the Soviet Union, but despite his global outlook President Kennedy was also responsible for ordering the disastrous Bay of Pigs invasion of Cuba in 1961 and for sending the first American troops to Vietnam to help fight Communist forces.

At the time of Kennedy's assassination Nixon was working as a partner in the New York City law firm of Nixon, Mudge, Rose, Guthrie, Alexander & Mitchell, where he specialized in corporate law. He was not attending many political functions.

It was during this period, when Nixon was essentially a private citizen, that the civil rights movement was picking up momentum. Sit-ins at segregated lunch counters were spreading through the South in the early 1960s. In the fifties black people had begun resisting the long-standing discriminatory practice of sitting in the backs of buses. Some challenged restrictive laws by demanding integrated schools. Although the protesters, led by Baptist minister Dr. Martin Luther King, Jr., among others, remained nonviolent in their actions, their opponents used rubber hoses, guns, and fireballs to try to stop them. On August 28, 1963, about 250,000 people marched on Washington to demand civil rights. Standing on the steps of the Lincoln Memorial, Dr. King proclaimed, "I have a dream." His dream of a country where blacks and whites would be able to live in equality inspired millions.

But that dream also made many people anxious. As the civil rights movement strengthened, new black leaders expressed their desire for power and supremacy rather than simply equality. In February 1964 Nixon told a group of Republicans in Cincinnati that he wanted to see "responsible civil rights leaders . . . take over from the extremists."[2] Although he did not at any point speak out against the need for greater civil rights, Nixon was able to sense that many white middle-class Americans were becoming increasingly nervous, and his comments were meant to reassure them that he understood the concerns of those voters most likely to support him politically in the future.

When President Lyndon B. Johnson took over the nation's highest office after Kennedy was shot, he pushed monumental civil rights legislation through Congress. Nonetheless mounting social and economic pressure in the ghettos sparked a race riot in Harlem in the summer of 1964. Other black ghettos were also experiencing outbreaks of racial violence. At that point the Democratic and Republican parties were polarized in their responses to the worsening racial confrontations. The Democrats proposed stronger social programs for poor blacks, whereas Republicans were more reticent and conservative. Many Americans feared that Communists were behind the civil rights demonstrations. The women's movement, which demanded equality in all areas of life, became more prominent around this time too. In 1963 the Equal Pay Act was enacted, granting men and women the right to equal wages for performing the same job.

By 1964 the civil rights movement and the women's movement had begun to join into the growing movement to stop American involvement in Vietnam. Under the 1964 Gulf of Tonkin resolution President Johnson had empowered himself to escalate military involvement in Vietnam without seeking approval from Congress. Under the Constitution only Congress is permitted to declare war, but the Gulf of Tonkin resolution did not refer to the military build-up as war. Vietnam became known as the country's "undeclared war," with many Americans questioning its legality as well as its practical and moral value.

Richard Nixon believed that it was important to protect Vietnam from neighboring Communists by sealing it off militarily. In 1964 he paid a private visit to Vietnam to find out what was going on. In 1965 he wrote, "The battle for Vietnam is the battle for Asia. If the United States gives up on Vietnam, Asia will give up on the United States and the Pacific will become a Red Sea."[3]

In 1964 the Republicans nominated Barry Goldwater to run against Lyndon Johnson in the presidential elections. Nixon considered Goldwater an extremist who was a political liability to the Republican party. Nixon saw himself as a centrist, and he had tried to build a coalition of supporters to challenge Goldwater for the nomination. He had a small group of wealthy backers and his hardworking, enthusiastic supporters, H. R. Haldeman and John Ehrlichman. But the Goldwater faction had grassroots support that had spread through the country, and the Goldwater campaign had been able to raise twelve times as much

Richard Nixon goes fishing alone in Fraser, Colorado, July 29, 1952.
(WIDE WORLD PHOTOS)

In Cleveland, Ohio, General Dwight D. Eisenhower and his wife, Mamie, watch Richard Nixon deliver the Checkers speech, September 23, 1952.
(BETTMAN NEWSPHOTOS)

Richard Nixon and his wife, Pat, watch the election returns in Los Angeles, November 4, 1952.
(BETTMAN NEWSPHOTOS)

General Dwight D. Eisenhower and his running mate, Richard Nixon, campaign in Chicago, August 11, 1952. (BETTMAN NEWSPHOTOS)

In Washington, D.C., Vice President Nixon embraces his daughters, Julie and Tricia, upon his return from Venezuela, May 15, 1958.

(NATIONAL PARK SERVICE)

Soviet Premier Nikita Khrushchev and Vice President Richard Nixon in the "kitchen debate," Moscow, July 23, 1959 (WIDE WORLD PHOTOS)

money as Nixon had raised that year. One Goldwater supporter began using computers to generate the largest political mailing list in the nation's history, enabling Goldwater to reach people he called "the silent Americans."

In the first primaries of 1964 Richard Nixon was a write-in candidate but he failed to get enough votes to be a serious contender. When Goldwater was officially nominated, Nixon decided not to join forces with those Republicans who opposed him. Instead, like the consummate party politican that he was, Nixon campaigned for Barry Goldwater. This paid off for him in the long run because conservatives who voted for Goldwater in 1964 later perceived Nixon as an ally rather than an opponent. In November 1964 Lyndon Johnson was elected with 61 percent of the popular vote and forty-four states of the electoral college.

President Johnson quickly devised a series of programs designed to wage war on poverty. He called it the Great Society and it included such programs as the Office of Economic Opportunity, which dealt with community action; VISTA, an organization like the Peace Corps that sent volunteers to poor sections of the United States; Head Start, a preschool program; and Medicare.

While many of his domestic programs were popular, Johnson's Vietnam policy was not. Increasing numbers of students, journalists, and politicians spoke out against the war. Demonstrations expanded in size and began to include middle-class adults as well as students and civil rights activists. The antiwar movement was becoming as much a part of the Great Society as Johnson's social welfare programs.

By 1966 Johnson's political base was eroding. In the congressional elections that year Republicans won forty-seven additional seats and while that did not constitute a majority, it signaled that voters were not pleased with the current social turmoil and Democratic policies. A 1966 Gallup poll found that 75 percent of people surveyed believed that the Communists were behind the antiwar and civil rights demonstrations. A 1966 Harris poll found that an increasing number of white people were afraid of racial violence. Nixon was able to hone in on these fears during the 1966 congressional elections when he campaigned for eighty-six members of Congress in thirty-five states. Nixon paid particular attention to the South, where the backlash against civil rights progress was strongest. Although he stated his support for existing civil rights legislation and the need to desegregate, he managed to present himself as sympathetic to white southerners' views. To defuse concerns about race, he urged voters to focus on what he called "issues of the future." His campaign efforts in 1966, which included raising between $4 million and $5 million for various congressional elections, reestablished Nixon as a Republican leader.

It was around this time that Nixon began publicly to challenge President Johnson's Vietnam War policy. When Johnson prepared to meet with South Vietnamese leaders in October 1966, Nixon urged the president to push for a "long-range program for peace and freedom in Asia." When Johnson and the South Vietnamese leaders issued a joint communique calling for a "mutual withdrawal," Nixon was critical. Johnson responded by calling Nixon a "chronic campaigner" and Nixon commented that he would not be silenced by what he called "the presidential temper."

During these turbulent times a small group of young activists resorted to radical antics to gain attention. A mischievous group of Americans, led by Abbie Hoffman and Jerry Rubin, created the Youth International Party, nicknamed the Yippie Party. Among their more amusing stunts was a demonstration to levitate the Pentagon building, which houses the Defense Department, in Washington in 1967. To show their contempt for materialism they tore up dollar bills and threw them onto the floor of the New York Stock Exchange, setting off a mini-riot and causing the exchange to shut down trading. Hoffman described the Yippie actions as protests against "hotbeds of social rest," meaning middle-class adult society. An outspoken opponent of the Vietnam War, Hoffman was aware that he was unpopular with the authorities. "It's not a popular job to stand on the street corner and say the emperor has no clothes on. But you measure a democracy by its dissidents. You don't measure it by its conformists." He said later that the turmoil of the 1960s was an "intergenerational civil war in which many parents believed that their children were being used by the Communists."[4]

During the long, hot summer of 1967, racial riots in Detroit, Toledo, Grand Rapids, and Nashville claimed 225 lives. About four thousand people were wounded as violence spread through the inner cities. The antiwar movement was becoming more confrontational. In the fall of 1967 a group of militant protestors attempted to shut down one of the army's induction centers. Young men were burning their draft cards to symbolize their disrespect for the war. Protesters were chanting, "Hey, hey, LBJ, how many kids did you kill today?" and police were using tear gas more frequently to break up demonstrations, which often drew hundreds of thousands of people.

Richard Nixon paid another visit to Southeast Asia in the spring of 1967, stopping in South Vietnam, Japan, Formosa (Nationalist China, or Taiwan), and India. He met with leaders in each country, tape recording his own meetings with a hand-held machine. Because of his willingness to go out into the field Nixon earned many people's respect as a foreign policy expert. As a result of his travels he was becoming more international in his outlook. In September 1967 he said, "Increasingly, we are seen as an old nation in a new world." He mentioned the need to enter into a dialogue with China. "During this final third of the twentieth century, the great race will be between man and change: the race to control change, rather than be controlled by it. In this race we cannot afford to wait for others to act, and then merely react," he wrote in the October 1967 issue of *Foreign Affairs*.[5] With that article and speech Nixon began to establish himself as a candidate for president in 1968.

He discussed the idea of running for office again with

his family at Christmas in 1967. Despite her dislike of politics, Pat agreed to support him. Tricia and Julie were enthusiastic. When he entered the New Hampshire primary in March 1968 Nixon found that his image as someone who had lost two big elections was a handicap. He regretted having said in 1962 that he was giving his last press conference. To rebuild his image Nixon concentrated on projecting an image of statesmanship based on his own trips to South Vietnam and Asia. At the beginning of the 1968 campaign he introduced his concept of "Vietnamization" as a solution to the unpopular war. Vietnamization meant that the United States would supply the weapons and aid but the Vietnamese would fight the war themselves.

Nixon had chosen to reenter national politics at a time when turbulence was at an all-time high. Thus far the 1960s had been a period of unprecedented change, especially for young people. The social protests that included the civil rights movement, the women's movement, and the antiwar movement had initiated a revolution of social values in which young people challenged existing authority and adults' rights to make the rules. Because of the post–World War II baby boom, during the second half of the decade there was a population of more than six million college students and more teenagers than at any other time in American history; the revolution's impact had a lot to do with sheer numbers. Long hair, flowered shirts, and bell-bottom pants were standard dress for young people—a far cry from the crew cuts and button-down collars of the older generation. Use of marijuana became commonplace and many young people experimented with hallucinogenic drugs such as LSD. One slogan was "Turn on, tune in, drop out." Sexual attitudes became freer and many colleges, in the face of student demand, began to relax their strict regulations about dormitory visiting hours.

Musicians such as Bob Dylan, the Rolling Stones, and the Beatles filled the air with lyrics that challenged authority. But the international youth anthem was a simple protest song called "We Shall Overcome." And the glowing freeform colors of psychedelic posters were indelibly juxtaposed with the somber images of dead and wounded in Vietnam.

Nineteen sixty-eight was the year that the movement of peace and love turned darker. The Vietnam War was costing the United States between $2 billion and $3 billion a month.[6] On January 31 the North Vietnamese launched what became known as the Tet offensive, a major military push that coincided with the beginning of the week-long Confucian holiday known as Tet. The tone of news reports from the Vietnam War began to change. In *1968 in America: Music, Politics, Chaos, Counterculture, and the Shaping of a Generation,* Charles Kaiser writes, "Just four days after Tet began, Lyndon Johnson called the enemy's military effort 'a complete failure.' At the end of *two months,* 214 Koreans, 3,895 Americans, 4,954 South Vietnamese troops, 14,300 South Vietnamese civilians, and (by American estimates) 58,000 Communist troops were dead: a total of 81,363 men, women, and children shot, blown up, or buried alive. . . . The homes of 821,000 South Vietnamese had been destroyed, so now there were 821,000 new refugees, doubling the total before Tet."[7]

The much admired and influential CBS News anchorman Walter Cronkite reported from Vietnam on the nineteenth day of Tet, "To say that we are mired in stalemate seems the only realistic, yet unsatisfactory, conclusion." President Johnson, who came to personify America's involvement in Vietnam, was reportedly devastated by Cronkite's new perspective and believed that if Cronkite was against the war, he, Lyndon Johnson, had no hope of holding the support of the American public. His health began to deteriorate as a result of stress and on March 31, Johnson announced, "I shall not seek, and I will not accept, the nomination of my party for another term as your president."

This opened the field for the Democrats. Johnson's heir apparent was Vice President Hubert Humphrey, formerly a senator from Minnesota, who had the backing of the mainstream Democratic party. Humphrey, however, was seen by many as representing a continuation of Johnson's Vietnam policy, and was jeered by young people carrying signs saying DUMP THE HUMP! and BRING THE TROOPS HOME. A columnist for the *New York Times* described his campaign as "long on delegates but short on enthusiasm." Coming up from the rear was another Democratic senator from Minnesota, Eugene McCarthy, who had announced his candidacy in November 1967. Although McCarthy, a soft-spoken intellectual, never actually came out and said he wanted to be president, he had managed to pick up momentum by campaigning on a strong antiwar platform.

McCarthy attracted thousands of young people dubbed the "children's crusade." They cut their hair, shaved their beards, and shed their flowered shirts for button-downs in order to appear presentable when they canvassed voters. After pulling off an amazing victory in the New Hampshire primary, McCarthy continued to pick up momentum around the country until Senator Robert F. Kennedy, the younger brother of John F. Kennedy and the attorney general in his administration, announced he was throwing his hat into the ring.

Kennedy's announcement threw both the McCarthy and Humphrey camps into disarray. The Kennedy mystique, which somehow conveyed youthful idealism, action, and glamour, had fascinated Americans since the presidency of Robert's brother. After his assassination in 1963 many Americans, especially young people, longed to find a leader who would recapture those qualities. Bobby Kennedy seemed to promise to carry on his brother's legacy in 1968.

Kennedy's passion was civil rights, and by 1968 the civil rights movement had reached a new intensity. Black pride was strong, bolstered by the slogan "black is beautiful." Although there were a number of influential and respected black leaders in the growing drive for racial justice and equality, perhaps the most prominent civil rights leader was still Dr. Martin Luther King, Jr., a gifted orator whose passion for equality was fueled by his compassion for those who suffered discrimination.

On April 3, King went to Memphis to support a strike by sanitation workers. The following day he met with supporters to plan a big march. Despite threats of violence, King vowed he would attend the demonstration. "I'd rather be dead than afraid. You've got to get over being afraid of death," he said.[8] Shortly before dinner he stepped out of his motel room onto a small balcony. A shot was fired from a window not far away and King fell to the floor; he died soon after in the emergency room of a Memphis hospital. He was thirty-nine years old.

Over the next few days riots broke out in 130 cities. Stokely Carmichael, a militant black leader, told people to go home and get a gun, warning that the white man was going to kill them. Rioting in Washington came within two blocks of the White House. City officials imposed a curfew from 4:00 P.M. to 6:30 A.M. Riot police took up positions around the White House lawn and machine-gun nests were set up. Eventually 65,000 National Guard troops were activated to calm things down in cities across the nation. After riots broke out in Baltimore, Maryland, Governor Spiro T. Agnew accused middle-class blacks of participating in a conspiracy to riot. Apparently this impressed candidate Nixon, who was looking to appeal to white conservatives.

Throughout the spring of 1968 civil rights protests, antiwar demonstrations, and student uprisings continued. An estimated 40,000 students participated in more than 221 large demonstrations at over one hundred colleges around the country. At Columbia University students took over five buildings, including the administration building, and similar campus unrest spread through Europe as well. In

Italy university students shut down more than twelve colleges. In Paris a young man named Daniel Cohn-Bendit, known as Danny the Red, led the takeover of the Sorbonne University. After a loosening up of Communist restrictions in Prague, Czechoslovakia, during the spring, Soviet tanks rolled into the center of the Czech capital in August, shutting down all forms of freedom of expression in that Eastern European country.

While the political turmoil continued, the Democratic candidates continued to battle in the primaries for their party's nomination. After McCarthy won the Oregon primary with nearly 44 percent of the vote to Kennedy's 39 percent of the vote, the media began predicting a McCarthy sweep. But on June 4, Bobby Kennedy won California. At Kennedy's hotel in Los Angeles people were singing "This Land Is Your Land" to celebrate his primary victory. Shortly after midnight Kennedy went downstairs to thank them. After encouraging all to look toward the next primary challenge he stopped in the hotel kitchen to shake hands with one of the dishwashers. It was there that he was shot. Kennedy died the next day. The man who had killed him was identified as twenty-four-year-old Sirhan Sirhan, a Jordanian who was carrying a newspaper clipping about Kennedy's support for Israel.

The funeral was held in St. Patrick's Cathedral in New York City. He was eulogized by his brother Ted Kennedy, who quoted Bobby as saying, "Some men see things as they are and say why. I dream things that never were, and say why not?" His coffin was brought to Washington,

D.C., on a special train. Thousands upon thousands of people lined the tracks to pay homage to him. For many, Bobby Kennedy's death, coming so close on the heels of Martin Luther King, Jr.'s, marked the end of hope.

Politically Kennedy's assassination created chaos in the Democratic party. Eugene McCarthy startled supporters by commenting that Kennedy had "brought it on himself" by openly stating support for selling weapons to Israel. In McCarthy's view, Kennedy's opinions had enraged Sirhan Sirhan to the point of madness. But McCarthy's poor judgment, as well as his seeming coldness and lack of sympathy, shocked many of his supporters and caused some people to back Humphrey instead. Some of McCarthy's staff wondered if he had a political death wish, a hidden desire to self-destruct instead of triumph.

As that tense spring unfolded into summer Humphrey's candidacy got another boost when the Republicans nominated Richard Nixon. Nixon was so fiercely disliked by so many people that Humphrey was sure he would attract "anti-Nixon" votes. "I've read of the new Nixon in 1952, in 1956, in 1958, and in 1968. I've never known one man that had so many political face-liftings in my life," Humphrey quipped.[9]

The Republican National Convention was held in Miami early in August. Antiwar protesters were planning major demonstrations at the Democratic National Convention, which was to be held later that month in Chicago. Perhaps because they did not hold the Republicans responsible for the government's Vietnam policy, the protesters stayed clear of the GOP convention. In his book *The Making of the President, 1968* Theodore H. White writes, "Boredom lay on the convention like a mistress." Nixon sauntered into the convention assured of winning the necessary 692 delegates on the first round of balloting. After accepting the nomination he staged the only surprise of the convention by choosing Maryland governor Spiro T. Agnew to be his running mate for vice president. Headlines all over the country blazed, SPIRO WHO? reflecting the relative lack of political experience in Nixon's running mate. Preliminary investigations into Agnew's background turned up one nugget of trivia: He had been voted one of the best-groomed men in America by *Men's Hairstylist and Barber's Journal*. He had also talked tough to blacks after King's assassination. Ironically rioting broke out in one of Miami's black ghettos during the Republican National Convention and four people were killed. Alabama governor George Wallace was a third-party candidate for president. General Curtis Emerson LeMay was his vice-presidential running mate. The candidacy of Wallace and LeMay appealed to white voters who felt threatened by both the spread of civil rights and growing racial violence.

Halfway across the country in Chicago, Democrats and antiwar demonstrators were gearing up for the Democratic National Convention. Huge billboards pronounced MAYOR DALEY, A FAMILY MAN, WELCOMES YOU TO A FAMILY TOWN. Mayor Daley's idea of family would turn out to be more like Adolf Hitler's than Bill Cosby's. The night before the convention, demonstrators who had been denied permits to camp in the city's parks were cleared out by policemen wielding clubs. The demonstrators taunted the police, calling them "pigs." When a *Newsweek* reporter showed his press card to a policeman, the cop cursed at him and beat him with a club. By the end of the night ten reporters had been clubbed and beaten.

According to Charles Kaiser's account in *1968 in America*, Mayor Richard Daley's tactics were merely the local version of some of the tactics being used by the federal government that year. The FBI and the CIA had informers in nearly all of the antiwar organizations. The CIA was conducting surveillance operations on American citizens. The CIA director, Richard Helms, noted that CIA surveillance reports had to be kept confidential because "the agency should not be reporting at all on domestic affairs of this sort." Daley had his own nationwide spy ring, the Chicago Department of Investigation. Daley claimed that his agents had infiltrated antiwar groups on both the East and West coasts. The FBI played its role in sabotaging the demonstrators at the Chicago convention by printing a phony list of people offering housing to protesters. Many people arrived in Chicago expecting to be able to stay at certain homes, only to find themselves sleeping on the streets. The army had dispatched a military intelligence film unit to the convention. Every day its footage was shipped to Washington for screening. So comprehensive was government infiltration at the Democratic convention that military officials estimated that one out of every six protesters there was really a government agent.

Although he had alienated some supporters, Senator Eugene McCarthy was still a leading contender one week before the Democratic National Convention when Soviet troops rolled into Prague, Czechoslovakia, on August 20 to quell a potential uprising. Instead of capitalizing on that event by making a strong statement that was sympathetic to the Czech people, McCarthy issued a statement saying, "I do not see this as a major world crisis." Several days earlier he had gone public with a list of people he would appoint to his cabinet. They included Coretta Scott King, the widow of Dr. Martin Luther King, Jr., as well as several prominent Republicans. Democrats who had worked hard for him were appalled. These two actions, coming in the wake of his chilling response to Bobby Kennedy's murder, effectively undermined McCarthy's credibility. Many people who have analyzed his actions believe that McCarthy sabotaged his own success for reasons that are not understood.

The mood in Chicago grew uglier and more violent as the convention progressed. CBS News correspondent Dan Rather was roughed up by a security guard on the convention floor. Yippie leader Abbie Hoffman was arrested for having the word *fuck* printed on his forehead. The comedian Dick Gregory staged an anti–birthday party for President Johnson, joking that Premier Aleksei Kosygin of the Soviet Union had sent a telegram to Mayor Daley requesting that riot police from Chicago report for duty in Prague. Inside the convention hall the Democrats fought over whether to include new peace proposals in their party's platform. After a heated struggle between the prowar and antiwar factions, those proposals were defeated.

Across the street in Grant Park ten thousand protesters staged an antiwar rally. When one student removed an American flag from a flagpole the police dragged him away. Another young man climbed up and tied a red shirt to the top of the flagpole. A full-scale riot broke out with the police using clubs, tear gas, and Mace to quell the protesters. The protesters threw eggs, rocks, pieces of asbestos and vinyl tile, and balloons, some of which contained urine or paint. One policeman was reported to have shouted, "There's a nigger over there we can get," whereupon a group of policemen charged at the black man and beat him up. The crowd chanted, "The whole world is watching." Right outside the convention hall hundreds of people were tear-gassed and beaten with clubs. "They're really getting scared now," said one policeman, grinning. South Dakota senator George McGovern commented that he hadn't seen anything this shocking since Nazi Germany.[10]

By the end of the evening of August 26, 1968, Hubert Humphrey had won the nomination with 1,761¾ votes. (Pennsylvania had a total of 103¾ votes, explaining the fractional vote.) Eugene McCarthy had 601. George McGovern, who had announced his candidacy two weeks before the convention, had received 146½ votes and the other candidates got a combined total of 100¾ votes. Upon leaving Chicago for his home in Minnesota, Humphrey said, "We ought to quit pretending that Mayor Daley did something that was wrong. He didn't condone a thing that was wrong. He tried to protect lives."[11] Two days later Humphrey took that back and said the police had over-reacted by beating up demonstrators. Less than one month after winning his party's nomination Humphrey was booed off the stage at a Boston rally. People carried signs saying MAYOR DALEY FOR HEART DONOR and DON'T HUMP ON ME. Whenever Humphrey tried to speak, people shouted "bullshit" and chanted "Chi-ca-go! Chi-ca-go!" (Richard Nixon was able to speak at Boston rallies without being heckled. In a strongly Democratic town like Boston, Nixon was unimportant compared to Humphrey, who represented the Johnson administration's Vietnam War policy.) Humphrey attempted to break from the administration's policies by making a televised speech in which he said he would approve a bombing halt in Vietnam. Johnson had warned him, "Hubert, you give that speech, and you'll be screwed."[12] For a while his defiance seemed to help the embattled vice president because many Democrats wanted to believe he would end the war. Overall, Humphrey's candidacy served only to fuel Richard Nixon's. Even when he ran a television ad about Agnew's being "a heartbeat away from the presidency," Humphrey was unable to pick up any significant momentum.

Shortly before election day, with Humphrey trailing Nixon by fourteen points in the public opinion polls, Johnson announced that he had ordered a halt to all air, land, and sea attacks on North Vietnam. "I have reached this decision in the belief that this action can lead to progress towards a peaceful settlement of the Vietnam War." Several days later the South Vietnamese rejected the Johnson peace overture. According to several accounts, some behind-the-scenes maneuvering by the Nixon camp had managed to persuade the South Vietnamese that if they waited until after the election they would get a better deal from Richard Nixon as president.

In addition to pursuing a campaign strategy that was geared toward making Nixon look better on television, his campaign team was actively pursuing behind-the-scenes contacts in the field of foreign policy. According to Seymour M. Hersh's account in *The Price of Power: Kissinger in the Nixon White House*, Henry Kissinger, originally a Democrat, was engaged essentially to spy on the Democratic peace effort and report back to the Nixon people secretly. Kissinger, a German immigrant who speaks with a thick accent, had been a professor at Harvard as well as New York's Republican governor Nelson Rockefeller's foreign policy expert during his own bid for the Republican presidential nomination. Because of his academic credentials, he had entrée into top Democratic circles and was able to ferret out inside information and pass it on to the Republicans. His strategy was to remain undercover so that no matter who won, he would get a top foreign policy job.

On the domestic front Richard Nixon focused on perfecting his television persona. His campaign managers tried to keep him from any extemporaneous encounters with reporters and they carefully staged all of his television appearances. One of his advisers said that "Nixon depended on a television studio the way a polio victim relied upon an iron lung." During one panel discussion Nixon was asked to comment on the charge that his views were based on expedience rather than conviction. His response: "I suppose what you are referring to is: Is there a new Nixon or is there an old Nixon? I suppose I should counter by saying: Which Humphrey shall we listen to today?" As the audience broke into thunderous applause, he added, "There certainly is a new Nixon."

For one thing, the "new Nixon" was no longer afraid to employ television consultants, many of whom had worked in the field of advertising. Masters of the sixty-second commercial, they found that packaging a political candidate was very similar to packaging a can of Campbell's soup; maybe easier, because the political "can of soup" could deliver its own lines. Nixon, noted one of these image consultants, had raised the use of the platitude to an art form. He had several image problems to overcome. Many people still thought of him as "Tricky Dick," the sore loser. He was the butt of many jokes. The comedian Mason Williams quipped, "This humble man has once again offered himself on the basis of his experience and I think we should accept him on that basis. After all, why go to the trouble of breaking in a new loser?"

Even Roger Ailes, the television consultant who was primarily responsible for packaging candidate Nixon, said frankly during the 1968 campaign, "Let's face it, a lot of people think that Nixon is dull. . . . They look at at him as the kind of kid who always carried a book bag. Who was forty-two years old the day he was born. They figure other kids got footballs for Christmas, Nixon got a briefcase and he loved it. He'd always have his homework done and he'd never let you copy." Putting Nixon on television was a problem because "he looks like somebody hung him in a closet overnight and he jumps out in the morning with his suit all bunched up and starts running around saying, 'I want to be president.' " But Nixon's media consultants put their personal views aside and were able to create a successful television campaign.[13]

On November 5, 1968, Richard Nixon was elected president of the United States. Although the preelection polls had predicted a wider margin of victory, the election was close. Nixon won 43.4 percent of the vote; Humphrey won 42.7 percent. Richard Nixon had won barely half a million votes more than his Democratic opponent.

CHAPTER EIGHT

The Presidency

AS PRESIDENT, RICHARD Nixon moved to isolate himself from the administrative operations of the White House. A loner by nature, he spent most of his time alone in the Oval Office, and as his first term progressed, he saw fewer people and came to rely almost exclusively on three: H. R. Haldeman, his former campaign manager; John Ehrlichman, Haldeman's best friend, who handled domestic policy; and Henry Kissinger, his national security adviser.

There are several accounts of life in the Nixon White House. Both *The Final Days* by Bob Woodward and Carl Bernstein and *The Palace Guard* by Dan Rather and Gary

Paul Gates describe the secretive, protective nature of the president's top three men, whom the White House press corps nicknamed the "Palace Guard." Less flattering were such descriptions as "All the King's Men," and the "Knights of the Woeful Countenance," a reference to Cervantes' Don Quixote. Since Haldeman, Ehrlichman, and Kissinger had German backgrounds, reporters sometimes referred to them as the "Berlin Wall" or "All the King's Krauts." Haldeman and Ehrlichman were dubbed "Hans and Fritz."

There is an anecdote about former president Lyndon Johnson's paying a visit to Richard Nixon in the Oval Office. Johnson was renowned for having a cluttered desk full of telephones with lines that went directly to various government agencies so that he could jab a button and reach anyone he wanted. Johnson was fond of picking up the phone to praise or castigate people personally. Apparently the former president was startled when he saw Nixon's desk. For one thing, it was a lot smaller than his had been. For another, it was a lot neater. But the most shocking thing, to Johnson, was that Richard Nixon had only one telephone with three buttons on his desk. "Three buttons!" Johnson exclaimed. "And just think, they all go to Germans!"

Haldeman and Ehrlichman surrounded themselves with eager, bright young men who were as close to clones of themselves as possible. All of them wore the obligatory white shirts and crew cuts. All of them were obedient, never questioning orders. Haldeman once wrote a letter to one of his aides that said, "Your job is to do, not to think." These bright young men of the Nixon White House were nicknamed the Beaver Patrol because they were "eager beavers."

Although Haldeman, Ehrlichman, Kissinger, and their subordinates were all committed to serving President Nixon, Haldeman was the closest to the president. It was Haldeman who sat outside Nixon's office doling out precious appointment time and restricting visitors. And it was Haldeman in whom Nixon confided his suspicions about certain White House staff members. Haldeman was so devoted to his boss that one of his favorite pastimes was showing home movies of Nixon to his friends. After the 1968 victory Haldeman's wife said, "Thank goodness he has found Nixon. Now Bob has something to devote his life to." This devotion included making sure that he ate the same thing as the president did for lunch every day: pineapple and cottage cheese. Compulsively neat and a workaholic to boot, Haldeman had a talent for using bureaucratic language when simple words would do. Press briefings became "information opportunities." Plans were always "implemented."

Haldeman's highest calling was overseeing President Nixon's image by making sure that all of his public appearances were tightly controlled. On one occasion a group of blind people visited the White House and knelt down to feel the presidential seal on the floor. Fascinated, Nixon himself got down on the floor to feel the presidential seal with the blind people. The White House photographers snapped away, delighted to have a picture of Richard Nixon doing something spontaneous. Haldeman was furious and ordered the film confiscated. Nixon's behavior was not "presidential," according to the chief of staff, and people should not be allowed to see the photographs. "Every president needs a SOB and I'm Nixon's," Haldeman sometimes growled.

Haldeman believed that "the key to an effective Richard Nixon is to keep him relaxed. The way to make [Nixon] accessible is to isolate him from the trivia and that's my job."

Bob Haldeman, his old college buddy John Ehrlichman, and, to a certain degree, Henry Kissinger stayed behind the scenes during the first few years of Nixon's presidency. Haldeman and Ehrlichman shunned publicity, preferring to use Attorney General John Mitchell and the outspoken Vice President Spiro Agnew as their mouthpieces. Both Mitchell and Agnew were fond of criticizing liberals, especially those whom they regarded as the liberal media establishment. Vice President Agnew achieved instant notoriety when he described the press as "effete snobs" and "nattering nabobs of negativism." The main goal of the Nixon administration was to shift American political opinion to the right, much as President Franklin Roosevelt had shifted it to the left. To this end, the Nixon team resorted to some of the old Nixon tactics. Attack the opposition and don't let the truth get in the way.

During his first term in office the men around President Nixon consolidated his power, extending the reach of the executive branch and isolating the president even from members of his own cabinet as well as from Congress. Particular attention was given to foreign policy as the president and his cunning national security adviser set up secret codes and "back-channel" communications systems with foreign embassies so that in the decision-making process they could completely bypass Secretary of State William Rogers and Secretary of Defense Melvin Laird.

Nixon had always been a loner and an introvert, and by the time he arrived in the White House those aspects of his personality had become more dominant. Rather than questioning whether it was a good idea to seal himself off from his cabinet and Congress as well as from the public at large, Nixon seemed to enjoy it. It gave him the privacy to express himself without fear of public reprisal. The darker side of Nixon's personality became more prominent. In his disturbing behind-the-scenes account of the Nixon White House, Seymour M. Hersh reveals that the man running the country expressed himself with cheap epithets and racial slurs. In the early months of his presidency Nixon unnerved Kissinger by making remarks about "Jewish traitors," and the "Eastern Jewish establishment," especially those Jews at Harvard, calling on Kissinger to back him up by saying, "Isn't that right, Henry?" Kissinger, himself Jewish, would back off nervously, saying, "There are Jews and Jews, Mr. President." Although Kissinger controlled his remarks at first, eventually he began leaking his opinions to the press. "You can't imagine how much anti-Semitism there is at the top of this government—and I mean at the top," he said.[1] In addition to his openly anti-Semitic remarks, Nixon referred to blacks as "niggers" and "jungle bunnies." And that's when he was sober. Although a few Jewish aides were made uncomfortable by Nixon's attitudes, most of the Beaver Patrol seemed to operate with blinders on except when it came to his drinking.

Nixon's drinking was a well-kept secret during his first term in office. Although Haldeman and Ehrlichman, both teetotalers, claimed that Nixon did not drink more than one or two highballs and simply had a low tolerance for alcohol, Kissinger, his chief aide Colonel Alexander Haig, and several other members of the foreign policy staff were very disturbed by the president's drinking. "We've got a madman on our hands," Kissinger and Haig reportedly told Secretary of Defense Melvin Laird. Kissinger's secret diary, which was kept in an electronically wired safe, had many references to the president's drinking.[2]

Richard Nixon's drinking behavior had first been noticed by his staff during the 1968 campaign. It was at that time a source of concern to John Ehrlichman, a Christian Scientist. Ehrlichman had even refused to work on the campaign unless Nixon promised to stop drinking. According to Ehrlichman, Nixon had kept his word during the campaign but his drinking increased after the election. According to one of Kissinger's staff, "Nixon drank exceptionally at night and there were many nights when you couldn't reach him at Camp David," the mountaintop retreat where presidents and their families often spend the weekend. After listening to Kissinger talk to President Nixon when he was drunk one night, one National Security Council staffer worried that the nation was at risk. What would happen if the Soviets staged an attack at night when the president was drunk? Particularly distressing were the weekends that Nixon spent in Key Biscayne, Florida, drinking with his friends Bebe Rebozo and Robert Abplanalp. "To the extent there was a problem it was very real in Key Biscayne," one staff member recalled. On one occasion an inebriated Richard Nixon stopped to admire an attractive woman and said to Kissinger, "She looks like she's built for you, Henry." This drunken, crass behavior was anathema to several White House aides, one of whom recalled feeling schizophrenic because of what he knew about the president's drinking problem, partly because of its seriousness and partly because of the White House paranoia about leaks to the press. "You go around taking it for granted that Nixon's nuts," the staffer explained, adding that this was a subject that was assumed to be forbidden when speaking to anyone outside the White House.

This obsession with secrecy was one of the main characteristics of the Nixon administration, and it soon led to the White House wiretaps. In May 1969 Henry Kissinger became the first White House staff member to wiretap his own employees. Kissinger was disturbed by a *New York Times* article describing the first secret bombing raid on Cambodia in March 1969. The article also indicated that these bombings were part of a new "get tough" policy intended to scare the North Vietnamese.

The secret bombing of South Vietnam's neighbor Cambodia was intended to help eliminate North Vietnamese training camps and hideouts along the Cambodian border with South Vietnam. Many Americans perceived the bombing as an escalation of the war and one way in which President Nixon was carrying out his policy of Vietnamization. The president and his national security adviser were enraged when the story leaked because Cambodia was a neutral country. The Cambodian leader, Prince Sihanouk, had requested U.S. air strikes against North Vietnamese Communist camps in his neutral country. Nonetheless Nixon and Kissinger knew that news of the secret bombings would anger other countries and inflame the antiwar movement. Nor would these reports help the American position in Paris, where peace talks with the North Vietnamese were underway.

Furious that the story had leaked to the *New York Times*, Kissinger called FBI director J. Edgar Hoover and told him that the White House would "destroy whoever did this if we can find him, no matter where he is."[3] In ordering the FBI to set up the wiretaps, Kissinger was equally careful to instruct the agency to conceal its business so that the wiretaps themselves would not become the subject of leaks. Further wiping his hands of the actual dirty work, Kissinger delegated the wiretapping assignment to his assistant, Colonel Alexander Haig. It was Haig who gave the FBI the names of people who worked for the National Security Council whose phones were to be tapped. He also gave them the names of reporters who were suspected of receiving confidential information. Haig also snooped on

National Security Council staffers to find out whether they were meeting with reporters. (In 1974, when Kissinger's role in the wiretapping was being investigated by the Senate Foreign Relations Committee, Kissinger maintained, "I would not say that I ever said to the FBI, please tap this individual. That was done by Haig." For his part, Haig said later that his conscience was clear. "I have absolutely no apologies to make. The wiretaps . . . were justified.")

Among the first people to have their phones tapped were Jewish staff members of the National Security Council. Insecure about his status in the Nixon White House, Kissinger believed that he could ingratiate himself with Haldeman, Ehrlichman, and Nixon if he demonstrated that he too was suspicious of Jews and was not going to protect these men just because he himself was Jewish. Then Kissinger had Haig order the FBI to tap the phones of several reporters working for the *New York Times*, the *Sunday Times* of London, and CBS News. There is some indication that President Nixon was not completely comfortable with Kissinger's wiretaps.[4] In a memo to Kissinger, Haig noted that "the president wishes to terminate them as soon as possible." Haig had urged that the wiretaps continue for at least two weeks, but some National Security Council personnel had their phones tapped for nearly two years.

Embroiled in their collusion, Kissinger and Haig began to stab each other in the back, with Haig claiming that Kissinger masturbated in his private office. Kissinger often scolded Haig in public, using language intended to humiliate him. Nonetheless the two of them were inseparable.

One aide joked that Kissinger kept Haig around "to testify in his defense at a war-crimes trial."[5] Most people realized that Kissinger needed a strong right-winger on his staff to fend off any criticism that he was not conservative enough; that may be why he tolerated the relationship. By the summer of 1969 the level of paranoia was so intense that Kissinger and Haig were worried that their own phones were being tapped too. Since they were the ones ordering the wiretaps, this new level of suspicion could have meant that Kissinger suspected Haig of tapping him and vice versa. Kissinger soon began to have his telephones "swept" to clear any possible wiretaps.

In the fall of 1969, as public opposition to the Vietnam War continued to grow and criticism of the White House grew with it, Kissinger ordered his staff to break all relations with the media. There was one exception. Kissinger had just been featured on the cover of *Time* magazine, and since he was pleased by the fawning coverage he had received, he would allow his staff to talk to *Time* reporters. The *Time* profile was one of the first articles that described Henry Kissinger as a "secret swinger"—bureaucrat by day, debonair socialite by night. Nonetheless the outright manipulation of people's fears, the snooping, and the back stabbing that characterized Kissinger's working style began taking a toll on his staff. The bright young people that he had hired started leaving the White House.

Unhappiness became too mild a word to describe the country's mood as the Vietnam War continued. In June 1969 hundreds of Brown University students walked out when Henry Kissinger was granted an honorary degree. In the autumn of that year antiwar protestors arrived at the gates of the White House carrying candles. One of Nixon's speech writers said he "almost threw up" when he looked out a White House window and saw his wife and children taking part in the candlelight vigil. As it was splitting the country, the Vietnam War was splitting American families—physically, mentally, and emotionally. On October 15, 1969, a quarter of a million demonstrators marched in Washington to protest the war. Hard at work on a speech that day, Nixon wrote at the top of a yellow legal pad: "Don't get rattled—don't waver—don't react."

On November 3, 1969, President Nixon gave a televised speech about Vietnamization from the Oval Office in which he announced that the United States would not leave South Vietnam until its people were able to defend themselves. He said "this first defeat in our nation's history would result in a collapse of confidence in American leadership." And he said that the prospect of global peace depended on the "moral stamina" of the American people. Then he appealed "to you, the great silent majority of my fellow Americans— I ask for your support. . . . North Vietnam cannot defeat or humiliate the United States. Only Americans can do that." With that well-scripted line, the term *Silent Majority* was born. The *Silent Majority* became a Nixon-era buzzword for those unidentified middle Americans who supported his policies on the Vietnam War as well as his views on other issues. A poll taken after the speech showed that 77 percent of those who had watched and heard his speech did support Nixon's views on Vietnam. Only 6 percent responded that they were opposed to him. The White House reported receiving no fewer than eighty thousand telegrams of support. However, one *New York Times* columnist picked up a curious conflict in the president's choice of words. Nixon had cautioned against defeat four times, and had spoken of disaster and humiliation twice each. The columnist believed Nixon was pessimistic about the war. But Richard Nixon believed that the Silent Majority speech had changed the course of events significantly. "Now, for a time at least, the enemy could no longer count on dissent in America to give them the victory they could not win on the battlefield," he wrote in his *Memoirs*. But on May 4, 1970, even the "Silent Majority" were shocked when National Guardsmen opened fire on student protesters at Ohio's Kent State University, killing four students. Two of those killed were demonstrating against the U.S. invasion of Cambodia. The other two were bystanders. Eleven people were wounded.

On the domestic front President Nixon grappled with the highest unemployment rate since the Eisenhower years (5.6 percent) and rising inflation. He attempted to fix it using an economic program reporters dubbed "Nixonomics," which someone described as "recession in the midst of inflation." First he hired Daniel Patrick Moynihan, a flamboyant Kennedy-era Democrat who in 1976 would be elected to the U.S. Senate from New York, to draft a Family Assistance Plan, but that fizzled. In addition, Moynihan fell victim to the crabby interoffice politics that plagued the Nixon White House. He soon left. In *The Palace Guard*, Dan Rather and Gary Paul Gates note that in "trying to fix recession and inflation, Nixon violated every economic principle that he had claimed to uphold." In 1970 he imposed wage and price controls in an effort to cut inflation. (He had them lifted during his second term and inflation and unemployment rose again.) But by the end of his second year in office Nixon had no legislative achievement to speak of. And having sealed himself off from his cabinet members and people of differing views, he became increasingly anxious and protective. Because he had come to the White House after a career in which he experienced humiliation and defeat as well as triumph, Nixon brought with him a personal emotional history full of hurt and distrust. Abetted by Haldeman and Ehrlichman, Nixon worried that his enemies—the Democrats, the antiwar protesters, and the media—were closing in. And his distrust of those around him grew.

According to Rather and Gates in *The Palace Guard*, the White House, increasingly driven to protect the presidency from its perceived adversaries, proposed establishing its own secret police force in June 1970. Made up of members of the CIA, FBI, and the White House staff, the force would be authorized to wiretap and commit burglary in order to tighten domestic security. The proposal for the secret police force stated, "Use of this technique is clearly illegal. It is also highly risky and could result in great embarrassment if exposed. However, it is also the most fruitful tool and can produce the type of intelligence which cannot be obtained in any other fashion." The controversial proposal was discussed and shelved.

In his State of the Union message at the beginning of 1971 President Nixon announced a $100 million grant for cancer research. But it was not the war on cancer that would earn him an irrevocable place in history. In February 1971 President Nixon decided to install a voice-activated tape-recording system in the Oval Office, the Cabinet Room, the Executive Office Building Presidential Office, the Lincoln Sitting Room, and Camp David. Taping systems were also installed in the phones of all of those sites. Nixon was not the first president to tape-record his conversations. In fact he had removed President Johnson's taping system in 1969. Johnson had even had a tape recorder in his bedroom, according to Nixon aides. Presidents Eisenhower and Roosevelt had also tape-recorded some of their phone conversations and meetings. President Nixon would later claim that he never intended for the tapes to be made public. Rather, he wanted to refer to them when writing his books. Haldeman and Ehrlichman were among the few people who knew of the taping system. Neither Pat Nixon nor the president's daughters were aware of it.

Nixon found that as soon as the taping system was completely installed he forgot about it and talked normally. But since Nixon only met with a handful of people, and since he cursed when he got angry or frustrated, the tapes would eventually provide a verbatim record of his siege mentality. According to Haldeman, Nixon's siege mentality extended to his own National Security Adviser. "Nixon realized . . . that he badly needed a complete account of all that they discussed. . . . He knew that Henry was keeping a log of those talks, a luxury in which the president didn't have time to indulge," Haldeman wrote, adding that Kissinger's opinions seemed to "change without notice." When, two years later, Henry Kissinger learned that his conversations had been tape-recorded he was furious, apparently because President Nixon had borrowed his favorite surveillance method and used it to better advantage.[6]

In June 1971 the *New York Times* began to publish the Pentagon Papers, a series of classified documents on the Nixon administration's secret Vietnam policy. Daniel Ellsberg, a former Pentagon official, was responsible for leaking the documents to the press. Disturbed by the Nixon administration's escalation of the Vietnam War, Ellsberg had photocopied top-secret Defense Department documents that described secret plans to escalate the war. As his sentiments against the Vietnam War grew stronger, Ellsberg decided to give the documents to the *New York Times*, which started publishing them on June 13, 1971. The Nixon administration obtained a temporary restraining order in an effort to suppress publication of the secret papers, but the Supreme Court overturned the order, ruling that "only a free and unrestrained press can effectively expose deception in government." In July 1971 Bantam Books published *The Pentagon Papers* in book form, based on investigative reporting by Neil Sheehan and written by

Sheehan, Hedrick Smith, E. W. Kenworthy, and Fox Butterfield.

Within one week of the Pentagon Papers' publication President Nixon activated a version of the secret police force first proposed one year earlier. The White House Special Investigations Unit was set up to "stop security leaks and investigate other sensitive security matters." Since they were ordained to plug "leaks," the White House called these special investigators "the Plumbers Unit." During a preliminary discussion of how the White House could retrieve some of the secret documents before they were published, Henry Kissinger asked, "Can't we send someone over there to get it back?" Although Kissinger claimed that he had no knowledge of the Plumbers Unit, this secretly taped conversation suggests that in fact he did. (While he managed to get through the Watergate investigation without himself facing serious investigation or having charges brought against him, Kissinger had been involved in these bizarre White House plots. Later an investigator listening to the tape of that conversation said he was shocked by Kissinger's attitude. "He was like one of the boys, talking tough. One says, 'Let's bring knives.' Another says, 'Let's bring bats.' And Henry pipes up, 'Let's bring zip guns.' I thought he might have been classier.")[7]

The White House Plumbers Unit was headed by Nixon's domestic policy adviser, John Ehrlichman. Ehrlichman hired Egil "Bud" Krogh, another Seattle lawyer; a former CIA agent, E. Howard Hunt; and G. Gordon Liddy, a former FBI agent who specialized in breaking and entering. Known as a wild man, Liddy had once, while arguing a case in court, fired off a pistol with blanks to make his point before a jury. Along with the Plumbers Unit, the White House drew up an Enemies List. Number one on that list was Senator Ted Kennedy of Massachusetts. Kennedy was considered Nixon's most serious political rival at the time. Number two was Daniel Ellsberg, who had leaked the Pentagon Papers to the *New York Times*. After that came various reporters who worked for major news organizations. Dan Rather was high on the White House Enemies List, as was investigative reporter Jack Anderson. As its first job the Plumbers Unit broke into the office of Daniel Ellsberg's psychiatrist in an effort to obtain confidential documents that would damage Ellsberg's public credibility. They referred to that break-in as "a bag job." Although the anti-Ellsberg operations were conceived as a general order from President Nixon to John Ehrlichman, Ehrlichman later claimed that he didn't know about the burglary in advance.

At the same time that he was installing his domestic espionage network Nixon was actively conducting secret foreign policy. He had the Chilean Embassy bugged in 1971. Chile's president, Salvador Allende y Gossens, a Marxist, had been freely elected despite millions of dollars funneled through the CIA to the anti-Allende opposition. Having failed to disrupt the Chilean electoral process, the Nixon administration was determined to disrupt the Allende government.

After a series of strikes and demonstrations funded by the CIA and American corporations, such as ITT, that had strong business bases in Chile, the Allende government was overthrown in a violent military coup on September 11, 1973. Allende was found shot to death. Although the official version was suicide, many believe he was assassinated by the military junta that replaced him. The Nixon administration supported the new regime because it was anti-Communist. The Chilean military junta imposed a police state, enforcing its rule through barbaric practices such as arresting and torturing thousands of citizens, many of whom were incarcerated in concentration camps in the southern part of the country near frigid Antarctica.

On a more positive front, Nixon had secretly dispatched Henry Kissinger to the Soviet Union and the People's Republic of China, and in February 1972 those missions yielded fruit when President Nixon became the first American head of state to visit mainland China while in office. It was a diplomatic and public relations triumph for the beleaguered president, and the White House made the most of it. Preliminary trips to China had ascertained that live television coverage of the historic "journey to peace" would be possible. Live satellite coverage of the trip was beamed back to the United States showing Nixon at the Great Wall of China and toasting his longtime enemies, Communist Chinese leaders Zhou En-lai and Mao Zedong. The People's Liberation Army Band played "Home on the Range" at a festive state banquet. The mood throughout the China trip was exhilarating, and that carried over when Nixon returned.

On May 20, 1971, before his China visit, President Nixon had announced that he and Soviet leader Leonid Brezhnev would sign a treaty to limit nuclear weapons. The talks leading up to the treaty were called SALT—Strategic Arms Limitation Talks. In exchange for the treaty the United States had promised the Soviets better trade deals, including more corn and feed for their livestock. The one stumbling block to success had been the maritime unions. Staunchly anti-Communist, the longshoremen had refused to load Soviet cargo ships. They wanted at least half of any grain sold to the Russians to be carried on American cargo ships. Ironically it was Nixon's strong anti-Communist stance that had propelled him to national prominence. Yet now he feared that anti-Communist sentiment might cause the SALT agreement to go sour. Once again Nixon and Kissinger were careful to report their triumph—a breakthrough in nuclear weapons control—while concealing the wheeling and dealing behind it. On May 22, 1972, fresh from the success of their China trip, Nixon, Kissinger, and their entourage arrived in Moscow for a historic eight-day summit that climaxed with the signing of the SALT treaty.

These major foreign policy achievements boosted President Nixon's popularity. Whereas he had been concerned in 1971 that he might not win his party's renomination for president, he sailed through the convention in 1972 and was up for reelection as the year drew to a close. But despite his significant gains in foreign policy, Nixon was still confronted with the overwhelming daily chaos created by the Vietnam War. In 1972 he had ordered that Hanoi be bombed in retaliation for a North Vietnamese push into South Vietnam. But behind the scenes he was frantically trying to set up negotiations that would lead to a settlement. To this end he had dispatched Kissinger secretly to Paris for meetings with North Vietnamese negotiator Le Duc Tho. Several weeks before election day Kissinger broke the news of his secret missions to Paris, announcing that "peace is at hand." It wasn't really, but coming from Kissinger it was enough to convince many people that the Nixon administration was prepared to end the war.

The success of the Paris peace talks, combined with the triumph of the SALT treaty and his historic trip to Beijing, resurrected President Nixon's reputation as a leader. Disenchantment with the Vietnam War and the economy did not seem as important to many people as his achievements in the global arena. However, the shadow of his secret plans to escalate the bombing in Vietnam and Cambodia, as revealed in the Pentagon Papers and other press reports, made many Americans uncomfortable. Although the intricate web of secrecy and suspicion that characterized the Nixon White House would not be revealed to the public until his second term of office, the momentum of betrayal and deceit had been set in motion by the wiretapping, secret taping system, and misadventures of the Plumbers.

Once exposed to public scrutiny, these presidential plots and misdeeds would seal Richard Nixon's fate.

CHAPTER NINE

Watergate

EARLY IN THE morning of June 17, 1972, five men were arrested breaking into the Democratic national headquarters in Washington. The Democratic National Convention was scheduled to be held the following month, and while no candidate had been officially chosen to run against President Nixon, South Dakota senator George McGovern was the front-runner. According to polls taken at the time, President Nixon had a nineteen-point lead over his most likely opponent. The Democratic offices were located in an office and apartment complex called the Watergate.

The burglary, which was reported in the media with little

fanfare, had far-reaching repercussions for the Nixon administration. According to an account published in *All the President's Men* by Carl Bernstein and Bob Woodward, the men arrested at 2:30 A.M. "had been dressed in business suits and all had worn Playtex rubber surgical gloves. Police had seized a walkie-talkie, forty rolls of unexposed film, two 35-millimeter cameras, lock picks, pen-size teargas guns, and bugging devices that apparently were capable of picking up both telephone and room conversations."

The five suspects included three Cuban refugees—Bernard L. Barker, Virgilio Gonzalez, and Eugenio Martinez—a mercenary named Frank Sturgis, and James McCord, a former CIA officer who was the head of security for the Republicans' Committee to Re-elect the President, known as CREEP. (Although CREEP was not an attractive acronym, a 1972 survey had found that people were turned off by the name Nixon. Ironically, in their effort to market the candidate and make him more appealing, Nixon's campaign organizers came up with an acronym that played to his enemies' perceptions of him.) Shortly after the break-in reporters questioned the burglars' attorney. One member of a group of journalists asked, "Is there something larger going on here that the public may or may not be aware of?" His response: "At this time these men are guilty of nothing. They haven't even been tried." He added that he did not know if there was "anything further involved."

The next day, after the burglary attempt was reported in the media, President Nixon publicly denied any connection with the break-in. "The White House has had no involvement whatever in this particular incident," he said. With his eyes fixed on the goal of winning reelection in 1972, Nixon's campaign manager, former attorney general John Mitchell, sought to deflect reporters' attention further by joining Nixon in denying any knowledge of the break-in. Asked whether a high Nixon administration official would "concede some knowledge or blame" in order to defuse the election-year competition between the two parties, John Mitchell snapped, "That's an absolutely ridiculous question. Why should they when they don't have knowledge? That's what we've been trying to get across to you."[1]

But it would be learned much later that four days after Mitchell's denial the secret taping system in the Oval Office recorded the following conversation:

NIXON: You'll uncover a lot of things. You open that scab. There's a hell of a lot of things and we just feel it would be very detrimental to have this thing go any further. This involves these Cubans, Hunt, and a lot of hanky-panky that we have nothing to do with ourselves. Well, what the hell? Did Mitchell know about this thing?

HALDEMAN: I think so. I don't think he knew the details, but I think he knew.

NIXON: So who was the asshole who did? Was it Liddy? He must be a little nuts.

HALDEMAN: He is.

NIXON: He just isn't well screwed on, is he?

HALDEMAN: No, but he was under pressure. . . .
NIXON: Pressure from Mitchell?
HALDEMAN: Apparently.

When the existence of this tape was revealed a year later, it became known as the "smoking gun" tape because it gave clear evidence that Nixon was aware of the implications of allowing details of Watergate to be made public. It also showed that Nixon and his chief of staff were quick to push the blame onto John Mitchell. The rest of the taped conversation between Nixon and Haldeman centered on getting the FBI to stop its investigation of the Watergate burglary, an act that, in effect, was an obstruction of justice. Mitchell resigned as Nixon's campaign manager on July 1, claiming that his wife wanted him to quit.

The smoke screen of blaming Mitchell and Liddy worked well enough during the 1972 election campaign, helped along by Nixon's decision to remain in the Oval Office as much as possible rather than face reporters and crowds. Nixon and his advisers decided that campaigning was not "presidential." One of the campaign tactics that was "presidential" was the wearing of American flags in lapels, an idea of Haldeman's. All White House staffers and campaign workers wore the flag pins, which, in Haldeman's view, sent a subliminal message that it was un-American not to vote for President Nixon.

The Watergate break-in did not become a major issue during the campaign. Democratic senator George Mc-Govern called the Watergate bugging incident "the kind of thing you expect under a person like Hitler."[2] And surprisingly Pat Nixon expressed her quiet concern about the Watergate break-in by confiding in a close friend, "If I were in charge of the campaign, I wouldn't be running it the way it is being run." Later Pat would blame herself for not voicing her objections more strongly. She told her daughter Julie, "I think I made a mistake in protecting Daddy too much and in giving in too much, but I knew he was busy and the war was hanging over us."[3]

On election night, November 7, 1972, while frenzied crowds chanted "Four more years! Four more years!" the man whom they were cheering sat alone in the Lincoln Bedroom of the White House. In front of a roaring fire Richard Nixon listened to his favorite music, "Victory at Sea." Surrounded by yellow legal pads, he wrote outlines and drafted memos. As the final returns came in, giving Nixon a 60.7 percent victory, he was saddened rather than jubilant. "I was not as upbeat as I should have been," he noted later, attributing his depression primarily to concerns about Watergate and the Vietnam War.[4] Despite Kissinger's October speech assuring voters that peace was at hand, the war dragged on and the Paris peace talks were blocked.

Then in December 1972 President Nixon ordered B-52s to bomb Hanoi and had the mines in Haiphong Harbor reactivated. (The mines had been laid in October 1972 but were not activated at first because the Paris peace talks were underway.) By the end of the month the North Vietnamese agreed to resume serious negotiations, and the bombing and mining were halted on January 15, 1973.

During this period both Harry Truman and Lyndon Johnson died, leaving no surviving former presidents. This reinforced Nixon's belief that it's lonely at the top. No one else on the face of the earth knew what it was like to be president of the United States.

As his second term got underway Nixon shocked his own staff by calling for all noncareer government employees in the executive branch to resign. This dramatic announcement included even his own cabinet. Nixon explained his bizarre proposal by saying that he did not intend to accept their resignations; rather, he wanted the gestures to be symbolic of a new beginning. Later he admitted this idea was a mistake. Pat Nixon was also disturbed by her husband's calling for employees to resign. Even more stressful to her was Nixon's increasing dependence on Haldeman to the exclusion of everyone else. At one point Haldeman urged Nixon to divorce Pat, claiming that she was a political liability. Nixon refused.[5]

Nixon also went on the offensive with the Democratic-controlled Congress, calling for major cuts in government spending. Members of the House and Senate were impatient with Nixon's budget-cut proposals and soon dismissed them. On January 11 the Senate Democratic Caucus voted to investigate the Watergate break-in and the conduct of Republicans during the 1972 campaign. The Senate Democratic Caucus had obvious political motives for probing Republican campaign conduct. But later that month, after a Washington jury found G. Gordon Liddy and James McCord guilty of participating in the Watergate burglary, the full Senate voted unanimously to investigate the Watergate incident.

The Senate Watergate Committee was chaired by Senator Sam Ervin, a North Carolina Democrat who was an expert on constitutional law. Ervin believed in the constitutional system of checks and balances that gave Congress the right to conduct a full investigation of possible abuses of power in the executive branch of government. In order to do that, Ervin issued subpoenas to President Nixon's aides. He demanded documents and challenged the notion of executive privilege, which the Nixon White House was trying to claim as a form of protection from releasing documents and information.

Until the spring of 1973, when the Watergate cover-up began to unravel, the Nixon White House had more or less successfully maintained an air of injured innocence about the Watergate burglary and the illegal use of campaign funds. But that stance became harder and harder to maintain as press coverage uncovered a trail of complicity that led directly to the Oval Office.

The prime movers behind those discoveries were two young *Washington Post* reporters, Bob Woodward and Carl Bernstein. Woodward and Bernstein had been chasing leads ever since the fateful morning of June 17. "Five men, one of whom said he is a former employee of the Central Intelligence Agency, were arrested at 2:30 A.M. yesterday in what authorities described as an elaborate plot to bug the offices of the Democratic National Committee here," their first story had stated. Bernstein had followed up with a report identifying four of the suspects as having CIA connections. The next day, under a joint byline, the reporters had filed a story identifying James McCord as a paid security consultant for CREEP. Up until that point the two young reporters had been extremely competitive, but suddenly a new camaraderie began to take form as Bernstein took it upon himself to rewrite Woodward's copy. Woodward conceded that his partner's version was better although they still argued over nuances of meaning.

The collaboration between Woodward and Bernstein is now legendary in American journalism. Had it not been for their persistent legwork and commitment, the course of American history might well have been different. Intrigued by McCord's connection to Nixon's reelection campaign organization, Woodward and Bernstein were stunned to find that two of the Cubans arrested had the same name in their address books: E. Howard Hunt. His address: The White House. After obtaining the confidential police log of the suspects' possessions, Woodward and Bernstein found "two pieces of yellow-lined paper." One was addressed to "Dear Friend Mr. Howard." The other was addressed to "Dear Mr. H. H." When Woodward called a friend who worked for the federal government to find out more, he was advised that this was just the beginning. The case was going to "heat up."

The reporters traced Hunt to the office of Charles Colson, special counsel to the president of the United States. Colson was an aggressive former marine who had bragged, "I would walk over my grandmother if necessary" to get Nixon re-elected. Hunt, who soon became a prime suspect in the case, turned out to be a former CIA agent. At the White House, press secretary Ronald Ziegler was trying to push the whole thing off as "a third-rate burglary attempt," but Democratic party chairman Larry O'Brien was enraged. "We learned of this bugging attempt because it was bungled," he said. "How many other attempts have there been and who was involved?"[6]

Identifying the cast in the Watergate drama turned into a twenty-four-hour-a-day job for Woodward and Bernstein, who also uncovered a paper trail of money that was funneled illegally into Mexico, then back into the coffers of Nixon's reelection campaign. Soon another Woodward–Bernstein article reported, "A $25,000 cashier's check, apparently earmarked for the campaign chest of President Nixon, was deposited in April in the bank account of Bernard L. Barker, one of the five men arrested in the break-in and alleged bugging attempt at Democratic National Committee headquarters here June 17." The General Accounting Office started its own audit of Nixon election contributions and found "hundreds of thousands of dollars in unaccounted cash . . . a slush fund of cash." This time there was no cute little puppy for Nixon to hide behind.

On August 29, 1972, President Nixon issued a statement from his home in San Clemente, California. John Dean, the White House counsel, had conducted a White House investigation into the Watergate incident and "categorically his investigation indicates that no one on the White House staff, no one in this administration, presently employed, was involved in this very bizarre incident. What really hurts in matters of this sort is not the fact that they occur, because overzealous people in campaigns do things that are wrong. What really hurts is if you try to cover it up." Woodward wrote a story pointing out that Hunt, Liddy, and Mitchell were among the people being investigated. All former White House aides, none of them was "presently employed" by the White House.

Woodward and Bernstein began to suspect that they too were under surveillance. As they worked on a story at Woodward's apartment one night, they turned the stereo up to full volume and passed notes to each other in case the apartment was bugged.

One of the most fascinating developments of the ongoing Watergate story was Woodward's cultivation of a highly placed source in the executive branch. The man, who insisted on secret meetings in the middle of the night in underground parking garages, became known as Deep Throat. (*Deep Throat* was a pornographic movie popular at the time and the nickname combined off-color humor with journalists' slang. "Deep background" means that a source is willing to talk to a reporter as long as his or her name is not mentioned in the story.) To this day, no one except Woodward knows his identity, if he existed at all. It was Deep Throat who verified that high-level Nixon officials were involved in the Watergate break-in and illegal money laundering schemes. He also gave Woodward firsthand information about White House officials who were participating in the cover-up. It was Deep Throat who allegedly told Woodward that Republican "intelligence-gathering activities" were more extensive than that one attempted bugging. And he pinpointed John Mitchell as the money man who controlled more than $300,000 for political espionage. White House "plumber" Liddy had gotten some of that money. So had Haldeman's assistant Jeb Stuart Magruder who, at the time of the break-in, was deputy director of CREEP.

As the reporters began to come up with more information about the role of the Nixon White House in the Watergate bugging, White House counsel John Dean spoke to Nixon about bribing the burglars not to talk. On March 21, 1973, the President's hidden taping system recorded the following conversation:

NIXON: How much money do you need?

DEAN: I would say these people are going to cost a million dollars over the next two years.

NIXON: We could get that. . . . What I mean is you could get a million dollars and you could get it in cash. I know where it could be gotten.

By the middle of April the president of the United States was being blackmailed. Hunt's attorney was demanding more hush money. A worried Dean returned to the Oval Office for another private meeting with the president during which he reported having the following conversation:

DEAN: I think that there's no doubt about the seriousness of the problem we've got. We have a cancer within, close to the presidency, that's growing. It's growing daily. It's compounding. It grows geometrically now because it compounds itself. . . . One. We're being blackmailed. Two. People are going to start perjuring themselves to protect other people and the like. And there is no assurance . . .

NIXON: That it won't bust.

DEAN: That that won't bust.

NIXON: True.

Dean told the president that he had been questioned by federal prosecutors. And while he was in the dark about the existence of Nixon's hidden tape recorders, he began to suspect that the conversation was being recorded. He noticed that Nixon was using a lot of leading questions, as if speaking for the record. That was one of the critical Watergate meetings. Later, when the special prosecutor subpoenaed the tape of that conversation, it was nowhere to be found. The White House claimed that the tape recorder had simply run out of tape. However, a Dictabelt recording that Nixon claimed to have made summarizing the conversation had also mysteriously disappeared.

On April 30, 1973, President Nixon announced the resignations of H. R. Haldeman, John Ehrlichman, and Attorney General Richard Kleindienst. Two weeks later FBI agents found wiretap records on seventeen people in Ehrlichman's White House safe. The president also fired John Dean, replacing him with New York lawyer Leonard Garment. He had agonized over the decision to get rid of Haldeman and Ehrlichman, but finally he had had to do it. The following day Nixon went on television to announce his decision. "The easiest course would be for me to blame those to whom I delegated the responsibility to run the campaign. But that would be a cowardly thing to do. I will not place the blame on subordinates, on people whose zeal exceeded their judgment and who may have done wrong in a cause they deeply believe to be right. In any organization, the man at the top must bear the responsibility. That responsibility therefore belongs here in this office. I accept it."

Several days later he went to Key Biscayne to unwind. He spent some time with his pal Bebe Rebozo, who was the perfect companion for Nixon because he could sit without speaking during the president's long, brooding silences. When he wasn't brooding or sulking in Key Biscayne, Nixon confided that he couldn't bear to think of the White House without Haldeman or Ehrlichman. He was reported to be drinking heavily.

Although he was no longer on Nixon's staff, it was Haldeman who stepped in to help Nixon reclaim some semblance of order. Haldeman suggested that Kissinger's aide Haig be made chief of staff. Kissinger was furious and threatened to quit. Nixon's secretary, Rose Mary Woods, snapped at him, "For once, Henry, behave like a man."[7]

On May 17, 1973, the Senate Watergate Committee began nationally televised hearings. Watergate burglar James McCord was the first to testify. He said that Howard Hunt claimed to have information that would be sufficient to impeach the president. That was damaging enough, but on June 25 John Dean took the stand protected by immunity. He read a 245-page statement in which he accused the president of trying to cover up the facts about Watergate. He said that after one of his private Oval Office meetings Nixon was "well aware of what had been going on regarding the success of keeping the White House out of the Watergate scandal." He also claimed that he had spoken on the phone with President Nixon at least thirty-five times about the Watergate cover-up and about paying hush money to the burglars.

Although the public did not know yet about the secret taping system at the White House, Nixon was listening to the tapes of his conversations with Dean in an effort to come up with a defense strategy. But the effort was exhausting. Nixon then came up with the idea of getting the FBI records on the Kennedy and Johnson administrations to find out who they had wiretapped. He would leak that information to the press so that the public could see that he wasn't any worse than his predecessors. Nixon's advisers weren't thrilled with that idea. For one thing, it showed that Nixon was using the FBI for his own political advantage. But he did come up with some dirt on John F. Kennedy that pleased him. During the Kennedy presidency Attorney General Robert Kennedy had authorized wiretaps on civil rights leader Dr. Martin Luther King, Jr.; on *Newsweek* and *New York Times* reporters; on a historian who wrote about Vietnam and knew Ho Chi Minh; and on the author of a book about a rumored sexual relationship between Kennedy and Marilyn Monroe. Upon reading that, Nixon felt superior to his old rival because he, Nixon, did not use wiretaps for personal vendettas. He told himself that he only used wiretaps for national security reasons. Feeling pleased with himself, he ordered his aides to leak the Kennedy wiretap records.[8]

But there was no way he could protect himself when Haldeman's former assistant Alexander Butterfield took the stand on Friday, July 13, and told the nation about Nixon's hidden tape recorders. Five days later the taping system was disconnected and on July 23 special prosecutor Archibald Cox, who had been appointed by Nixon's attorney general Elliott Richardson, subpoenaed nine of the tapes, claiming that they would provide evidence of criminal actions on the part of Nixon's aides. The embattled president refused to turn them over, citing executive privilege. Those tapes contained personal revelations from heads of state as well as White House officials, he insisted. Pat Nixon urged him to burn all the tapes immediately. Nixon insisted that handing over the tapes would violate the confidence of those who had met with him in private. He was unable to see that the very existence of his hidden tape recorder was itself a violation of confidence. An independent judge, John Sirica of the United States District Court in the District of Columbia, ruled in Cox's favor.

As the battle for the tapes raged through the summer of 1973, Vice President Spiro Agnew was under investigation for having accepted illegal cash payoffs over the years. Agnew resigned from office on October 10. Nixon chose

President Richard Nixon takes the oath of office on January 20, 1969, while Pat Nixon looks on. (NATIONAL ARCHIVES)

President Nixon talks on the telephone.
(NATIONAL ARCHIVES)

President Nixon smiles for the camera.
(NATIONAL ARCHIVES)

President and Mrs. Nixon at the Great Wall of China in 1972 (NATIONAL ARCHIVES)

President Nixon and Vice President Spiro Agnew at the 1972 Republican National Convention

(NATIONAL ARCHIVES)

President and Mrs. Nixon wave to the crowds in Washington, D.C., on his second inauguration as president, January 20, 1973.

(NATIONAL ARCHIVES)

John Ehrlichman (left), Henry Kissinger (center), and H. R. Haldeman (right) in the Oval Office with President Nixon (lower right)

(NATIONAL ARCHIVES)

President Nixon takes a walk with National Security Adviser Henry Kissinger. *(NATIONAL ARCHIVES)*

AS TO SEPARATION OF POWERS —

CONGRESS HAS BEEN PROVEN IRRESPONSIBLE.

AS TO FISCAL INTEGRITY —

CONGRESS HAS BEEN PROVEN IRRESPONSIBLE.

AS TO LOBBYING FOR SPECIAL INTERESTS —

CONGRESS HAS BEEN PROVEN IRRESPONSIBLE

AS TO LEAKING CLASSIFIED DOCUMENTS —

CONGRESS HAS BEEN PROVEN IRRESPONSIBLE.

THEREFORE IT HAS BEEN PROVEN THAT CONGRESS IS GUILTY OF EVERYTHING.

THE CONGRESS IS UNDER ARREST.

NOW WE COME TO THE MEDIA

©1973 JULES FEIFFER

Now we come to the media.
April 15, 1973.
(UNIVERSAL PRESS SYNDICATE)

President Nixon delivers his
resignation speech, August 8,
1974.   (NATIONAL ARCHIVES)

Vice President Gerald Ford (left) and his wife, Betty (second from left), escort President and Mrs. Nixon from the White House after President Nixon's resignation from office on August 9, 1974. (NATIONAL ARCHIVES)

FEIFFER

I ADVISED THE PRESIDENT ON HOW TO TOUGH IT OUT WITH GORBACHEV WITHOUT WEAKENING HIS HOLD ON POWER.

I CONSULTED WITH SECRETARY BAKER IN REGARD TO THIRD WORLD DEBT AND THE JAPANESE.

I GAVE THE CIA THE BENEFIT OF MY EXPERTISE ON INTERNATIONAL TERRORISM.

I BRIEFED MY ISRAELI FRIENDS ON HOW TO SHAFT THE PALESTINIANS WITHOUT ANTAGONIZING THE ADMINISTRATION.

I MET WITH COLONEL NORTH ON HIS POLITICAL FUTURE.

I PHONED A FEW MEDIA CONTACTS ON OUR OPTIONS IN CENTRAL AMERICA.

Nixon is forever. February 5, 1989.   *(UNIVERSAL PRESS SYNDICATE)*

Michigan congressman Gerald Ford as vice president. Although the courts had ruled in his favor, special prosecutor Archibald Cox still had not received any of Nixon's tapes. On October 20 Cox held a press conference in which he said, "You remember when Andrew Jackson wanted to take deposits from the Bank of the United States and his secretary of the treasury wouldn't do it. He fired him and then he appointed a new secretary of the treasury, and he wouldn't do it, and he fired him. And finally he got a third who would. That's one way of proceeding." Cox said that he planned to continue fighting for the tapes in court and that he would not step down. He added that he might file a motion to have President Nixon held in contempt of court if he did not hand over the tapes.

That same evening, Saturday, October 20, 1973, Nixon responded by ordering Attorney General Elliott Richardson to fire his special prosecutor. He said that if he let Cox threaten him, the Russians would think he was weak. "Brezhnev wouldn't understand if I didn't fire Cox after all this," he told Richardson.[9] Richardson refused Nixon's presidential command to fire the special prosecutor. Nixon then accused him of failing to act in the public interest. "Maybe your perception and my perception of the public interest differ," Richardson retorted. The next man down the line was the deputy attorney general, William Ruckelshaus. He too refused Nixon's order to fire Cox. Richardson and Ruckelshaus resigned in a series of events that became known as the "Saturday Night Massacre." The solicitor general, Robert Bork, the third in command at the Justice Department, became acting attorney general. He finally signed the order to fire special prosecutor Archibald Cox. At Alexander Haig's request, Bork drew up a list of candidates to replace Cox. Haig selected Leon Jaworski, a prominent Houston attorney who had served as special prosecutor in 1962 during the Kennedy administration. Haig reasoned that because of Jaworski's strong connections with Texas Democrats, he would appear nonpartisan and would easily be confirmed by the Senate Judiciary Committee. Although Jaworski did not want the job at first, he insisted on a guarantee from Haig that he would be allowed the independence he needed to conduct a proper investigation.

Three days later congressmen introduced forty-four bills concerning Watergate. Twenty-two of those bills called for impeachment proceedings. As Jaworski began to study the Watergate records, Nixon's lawyers became convinced that the president could not survive politically and began urging him to resign. He refused.

In November Nixon's lawyers testified in court that the tape of Nixon's meeting with Dean on April 15, 1973, was indeed missing, along with the Dictabelt summary of their conversation. During that session John Dean allegedly had described the "cancer in the presidency." What they didn't tell Judge Sirica was even more revealing: President Nixon had proposed making a new tape of that April 15 session, which would have been fabricating evidence.[10] Several days later the White House dropped another bombshell: The tape of a conversation recorded on June 20, 1972, had a gap that was eighteen and a half minutes long. During that conversation, which occurred three days after the Watergate break-in, Nixon and Haldeman had discussed the burglars' arrests. The gap appeared to have been erased. Nixon's secretary, Rose Mary Woods, claimed to have accidentally wiped out four or five minutes when she was transcribing it, but that failed to explain how eighteen and a half minutes were missing. Although he continued to refuse to turn over the tapes to investigators, Nixon had proposed turning over selected transcripts that he planned to edit in order to delete expletives and other material that he considered damaging.

On November 17 Nixon held a news conference designed to help him regain credibility. Reporters noticed that he seemed disoriented. He referred to himself as "he" and, regarding Haldeman and Ehrlichman, said "I hold that both men and others who have been charged are guilty until we have evidence that they are not guilty." Questioned about having paid less than $1,000 in taxes in 1970 and 1971, Nixon rambled on in a disconnected way about his finances in the year 1960. But he pulled himself together to make this final statement:

> In all of my years of public life I have never obstructed justice. And I think too that I could say that in my years of public life, that I welcome this kind of examination, because people have got to know whether or not their president is a crook. Well, I am not a crook.

CHAPTER TEN

The Final Days

SEVERAL DAYS LATER President Nixon faced the press again. CBS News White House correspondent Dan Rather asked, "What do you think when you hear people want you to resign or be impeached?"

"Well, I'm glad I don't take the vote in this room," Nixon snarled. He was becoming unraveled on television. Just as his television appearance had caused him to lose the presidency in 1960, the camera's "eye that never blinks" was once again hurting his credibility.

With the strain showing in his face, President Nixon delivered his annual State of the Union address on January

30, 1974. The prepared text touched on fighting in the Middle East, inflation, and states' rights. It made no mention of Watergate. But before leaving the podium Nixon broke from his text to say, "I have no intention whatever of ever walking away from the job that the people elected me to do for the people of the United States." His supporters in Congress gave him a standing ovation.

As he had throughout his political career, Nixon continued to attract fiercely loyal fans as well as opponents. One Nixon supporter, Rabbi Baruch Korff of Providence, Rhode Island, organized the national Citizens' Committee for Fairness to the Presidency. At a White House meeting Korff explained that he had been "offended" by the Watergate hearings because Senator Sam Ervin, who chaired the investigating committee, had apparently misquoted from the Bible.

"He's a nice man. He was just doing his job," replied President Nixon, referring to Senator Ervin.

Rabbi Korff responded by telling the president that he should have destroyed the tapes in order to protect the privacy of the people whose conversations had been recorded without their knowledge. But Korff and other supporters of the president were in the minority. As Watergate continued to unravel, Richard Nixon did too. The president was drinking heavily and often telephoned his chief of staff in the middle of the night. Sometimes Nixon started drinking in his office in the afternoon with his friend Bebe Rebozo. After a long night Nixon sometimes didn't get back to his desk until noon the next day. He had wild mood swings, from extreme sadness to manic joy. Sometimes he said that he would never leave the office of the presidency. At other times he spoke of resigning. Aides around him simply expressed the concern that Watergate was draining so much of his energy that he could no longer effectively lead the country.[1]

On March 1, 1974, a grand jury indicted White House aides H. R. Haldeman, John Ehrlichman, Charles Colson, John Mitchell, and several others in the Watergate cover-up. The jury cited Richard Nixon as an unindicted co-conspirator. In April the House Judiciary Committee subpoenaed forty-two tapes. The House Judiciary Committee, as the committee with the constitutional power to do so, was considering whether or not Richard Nixon should be impeached. The committee had started its work after the Saturday Night Massacre when twenty-two resolutions of impeachment had been introduced in the House of Representatives. Nixon decided that instead of handing over the tapes, he would supply the committee with edited transcripts of the conversations that were recorded. Diane Sawyer, a Nixon press aide, was one of the people charged with editing the curse words out of the transcripts. (Sawyer later became a correspondent for CBS News. Because of her loyalty to Nixon, Sawyer's hiring would become a source of irritation for many veteran correspondents, including Dan Rather, who was himself on Nixon's White House Enemies List.) Nixon released more than 1,200 pages of heavily edited transcripts, but Leon Jaworski, the new Watergate special prosecutor, still demanded sixty-four of the original tapes. The White House countered by appealing the subpoena. Nixon's lawyers lost that round and the special prosecutor went to the Supreme Court. Seeking to escape from his problems at home, Nixon visited Egypt in June. He came back to Washington, then went to Moscow for what he hoped would be a repeat success of his 1972 summit with Brezhnev. This time, though, the Soviets knew that Nixon was on the way out. There were no arms deals, just a minor agreement to continue negotiating. At a farewell toasting ceremony Nixon referred to his "personal relationship" with Brezhnev, but the Soviet leader was unresponsive. When his plane landed in Maine, Nixon gave a speech that made the trip sound better than it had been. "The process of peace is going steadily forward," he said. Avoiding Washington, Nixon went directly to Key Biscayne.

On July 24 the Supreme Court ruled unanimously that Nixon had to surrender the sixty-four tapes subpoenaed by the special prosecutor. It was believed that the tapes would answer the big question: What did the president know and when did he know it? Nixon then became concerned about another one of the tapes in question, that of a meeting between himself and Haldeman on June 23, 1972, less than a week after the break-in and several days after the eighteen-minute meeting that disappeared from the tape:

HALDEMAN: Now, on the investigation, you know, the Democratic break-in thing, we're back in the problem area, because the FBI is not under control. They've been able to trace the money, not through the money itself but through the bank, you know, sources, the banker himself. And it goes in some directions we don't want it to go.

Without a doubt, Nixon knew. Combined with the "smoking gun" tape, that conversation revealed that he knew about the break-in. He knew about the cover-up. And he knew a lot sooner than he had publicly claimed. President Richard Nixon had lied.

On July 27 the House Judiciary Committee passed the first of three articles of impeachment. It accused Nixon of obstruction of justice in trying to cover up the Watergate burglary. This was followed by the second article of impeachment, passed on July 29, which accused the president of "repeatedly violating the constitutional rights of citizens" and of abusing his power. The third article of impeachment, voted in on July 30, meant that when Congress reconvened in mid-August it would vote to impeach President Nixon.

Nixon, who had never been a great sleeper, was now a chronic insomniac. He didn't make it to scheduled meetings some mornings because he had been awake for most of the night. When he learned that John Ehrlichman received a prison sentence for helping to plan the White House Plumbers' raid on Daniel Ellsberg's psychiatrist's office, Nixon spent much of the night venting his rage. He refused to listen to any discussion of his future options. In drawing up those options—which included Nixon's remaining in office and fighting the impeachment proceedings in a Senate trial—chief of staff Alexander Haig looked into the possibility that Nixon could grant himself a presidential pardon. It had never been done, but no president in United States history had found himself in Nixon's position. Legally it was possible. If Nixon resigned, the incoming president could pardon him too.

On August 2, 1974, David Eisenhower, the president's son-in-law, met with Bebe Rebozo. They discussed a new investigation pertaining to Watergate. The committee had uncovered a $100,000 cash contribution to Rebozo for Nixon's reelection. The cash had come from the reclusive billionaire Howard Hughes. Even though he was himself embroiled in hearings and meetings with attorneys, Rebozo seemed more concerned about his friend, and for the first time he raised the possibility of Nixon's resigning. Knowing how close the two men were, the president's son-in-law realized that Rebozo was telling him that resignation was something Nixon was considering. He and his wife, Julie Nixon, were now practically living at the White House, and Watergate consumed their lives. Both Julie and Tricia defended their father and refused to listen to any mention of possible wrongdoing, which was becoming a source of tension in Julie and David's marriage. It was also affecting David's ability to concentrate in law school. As a more objective observer of the Nixon family, David Eisenhower said that he had expected "Mr. Nixon to go bananas." His father-in-law seemed so depressed at times that Eisenhower was concerned he might commit suicide.

That night Nixon summoned David to the Lincoln Sitting Room. Even though it was the middle of August, Nixon was seated in front of a blazing fire. At the same time the air conditioner was turned up full blast. Bebe Rebozo was with him. Nixon sat there staring into the fire and for a few minutes did not acknowledge the young man's presence. Finally he said, "It's over. We've got to decide by Monday night whether to get out of here." Nixon's eyes were glazed, as if tranquilized, and he was sadder than David had ever seen him. When he spoke about resigning, he would trail off in a disconnected manner. From time to time he said that he would fight because resignation would allow his enemies to triumph. But there was no fire or conviction in his voice.[2]

Julie, who had spoken to her father minutes before David arrived, had gone into her mother's bedroom to tell Pat the news. "A look of alarm spread across her face," Julie wrote in her book *Pat Nixon: The Untold Story*. Pat asked why and her daughter explained that he had to or he would be impeached. "Her mouth began to tremble. We embraced for a moment, our arms around each other very lightly," Julie wrote. When they pulled apart, she saw the tears in her mother's eyes. "For me, those tears that were shed so briefly were perhaps the saddest moment of the last days in the White House."[3]

"Daddy's not a quitter," Julie told Nixon loyalists the

following day. She was trying to convince them to back him if he chose to fight it out. The president's speech writer, Patrick Buchanan, said that although he empathized with Nixon's desire to stay in office, "it's a straight road downhill." He added, "The problem is not Watergate or the cover-up. It's that he hasn't been telling the truth to the American people. The president can't lead a country he has deliberately misled for a year and a half."[4]

On the morning of August 6, 1974, President Nixon told his cabinet that Watergate was "one of the most asinine things that was ever done," adding, "I'll take whatever lumps are involved." He claimed that his lawyers had told him he had not obstructed justice and had committed no offense deserving of impeachment. "If there were, I wouldn't stay in this office one minute." He claimed to have mishandled the intitial investigation into the break-in because of his concern with national security. "The CIA and the FBI were at loggerheads. I sought to act," he said.

Vice President Gerald Ford spoke up. "I'm in a difficult position. I share your view that the whole episode is a real tragedy." He declined further comment because his own self-interest was involved. But then he spoke bluntly. "Sure, there will be impeachment. I can't predict the Senate outcome." He praised Nixon for producing "the finest foreign policy this country has ever had" and said he supported Nixon's anti-inflation policy.

That afternoon Tricia's husband, Ed Cox, told a leading Republican senator that his father-in-law planned to resign. He said that although he and David Eisenhower believed this to be the wisest course of action, they were unable to persuade their wives. As a member of the Nixon family, Cox was concerned about his father-in-law's mental health, which appeared to be cracking. He revealed, "The president was up walking the halls last night, talking to pictures of former presidents, giving speeches and talking to the pictures on the wall."[5]

In the White House Nixon met with his staunch supporter Rabbi Korff. Korff did not want Nixon to resign. The president now said that he had to leave office or else "foreign affairs might suffer irreparable harm." Not only that, his staying in office would polarize the country. As he left the White House, Korff told reporters, "Richard Nixon will go down in history as the greatest president of the century."

The following morning the "greatest president of the century" was morbidly talking about death and suicide with his chief of staff, Alexander Haig. (Haig had been feeling so overwhelmed by the president's depressions that conservative senator Barry Goldwater had told him, "You look like death warmed over.") Nixon told Haig, "You fellows, in your business, you have a way of handling problems like this. Someone leaves a pistol in a drawer." He added sadly, "I don't have a pistol." Alarmed, Haig ordered the president's physicians to deny him tranquilizers and sleeping pills. He said that he wasn't merely concerned with the possibility of suicide. He was also worried about the president's ability to function and make decisions that affected the country. In Haig's view, President Nixon was as disturbed as Captain Queeg, the bizarre character in

Herman Wouk's *Caine Mutiny* whose ship had been taken over because he could no longer function. Haig understood that, in Nixon's view, suicide might be seen as a death with honor. If he killed himself, he would not cause the American people any more suffering. But Haig believed it was his duty to prevent that suicide.[6]

At dinner that evening Nixon raised the subject of the resignation with his family. He reminded them how pleasant it would be to live in California when the ordeal was over. Later that evening he called for Henry Kissinger to visit him in the Lincoln Sitting Room where he was drafting his resignation speech. Kissinger, who had been appointed secretary of state, was glad that Nixon was going to resign. He believed that the president was mentally incapacitated to such a degree that a nuclear war might erupt. He was shocked that Watergate—in Kissinger's view, a minor domestic scandal— had blown up into something with worldwide repercussions. While he was relieved that Nixon would be leaving, Kissinger was also angry. Watergate had interfered with his foreign policy plans. Nixon was sitting in front of the fireplace drinking when Kissinger arrived. They sat together swapping stories about their triumphs: China, Moscow, the Middle East. Nixon became weepy and asked Kissinger, "Will history treat me more kindly than my contemporaries?" His secretary of state assured him that when Watergate was over, Nixon would be remembered for his foreign policy achievements. Nixon cried. Embarrassed, Kissinger kept talking but Nixon was crying uncontrollably. "Henry," he said. "You're not a very orthodox Jew and I am not an orthodox Quaker, but we need to pray."

In *The Final Days*, Bob Woodward and Carl Bernstein describe what happened next:

> Nixon got down on his knees. Kissinger felt he had no alternative but to kneel down, too. The president prayed out loud, asking for help, rest, peace, and love. . . . Kissinger thought he had finished. But the President did not rise. He was weeping. And then, still sobbing, Nixon leaned over and struck his fist on the carpet, crying, 'What have I done? What has happened?'

Kissinger leaned over and held Nixon as he would a child. Again and again he repeated how much Nixon had accomplished. When Nixon got to his feet, he collected himself and poured another drink. (Although this version of events has been disputed, Nixon himself later confirmed that it took place when he was interviewed by British television personality David Frost in March 1977.)

With the atmosphere calmed down, Kissinger began proposing options for Nixon's future. He might become a special ambassador. An adviser. A consultant to governments. Later Kissinger described that session as "the most wrenching thing I have ever gone through in my life."[7] That night the president phoned Kissinger. He was practically incoherent as he begged, "Henry, please don't ever tell anyone that I cried and that I was not strong."

On August 8, 1974, President Richard Nixon went on

television to announce his resignation. "I have never been a quitter. To leave office before my term is completed is abhorrent to every instinct in my body. But as president I must put the interests of America first. Therefore, I shall resign the presidency at noon tomorrow."

After another sleepless night Richard Nixon strolled into the White House kitchen to talk to the chef. "I've eaten all over the world, but yours is the best," he told him. Looking over to the chef's assistant, Nixon added, "Tell Mr. Ford to hang in there and fight."

There remained only the task of composing his resignation letter. According to the Constitution, in order for a president to resign, he need only notify the secretary of state in writing. Nixon's letter to Kissinger was brief: "Dear Mr. Secretary, I hereby resign the office of president of the United States."

At 9:00 A.M. the staff of the White House gathered to say good-bye to the First Family. "I'm sorry to leave," Nixon told them. "This house has a great heart which comes from you who serve. There is only one White House. You are here to say good-bye to us. And we don't have a good word for it in English but the best is *au revoir*. We'll see you again."

Julie and Tricia were crying. Soon it was time for President Nixon's last televised appearance. Pat was appalled that cameras were going to record the shame of their final day in the White House. But to Nixon it was another opportunity to give a speech. He started by explaining that his remarks would be spontaneous. Then he thanked his staff for the sacrifices they had made in order to serve him. He described his father's early career as a streetcar conductor, farmer, and grocer. He described his mother as a saint. (One of his aides made a lot of money that day because he had bet several people that Nixon would not be able to give his farewell speech without mentioning his mother.) As he got to the end of his remarks Nixon started to shake and some members of the staff were afraid he wouldn't make it. "Always remember, others may hate you—but those who hate you don't win unless you hate them, and then you destroy yourself," he said.

The applause was tremendous. Many people in the room were crying. Typically Pat appeared to hold her emotions in check while her daughters openly expressed theirs. (Several nights earlier through the wall of the Oval Office, a White House aide had heard her speak to Nixon. "You have ruined my life," Pat had muttered.)[8]

"Good Luck, Mr. President," Nixon greeted Vice President Ford, and they shook hands. At the steps of the helicopter Ford made an effort to be amiable. "Drop us a line if you get the chance. Let us know how you are doing," he said. Nixon thought it was a strange way to say good-bye.

Richard and Pat Nixon and Tricia and Ed Cox walked to the helicopter on the White House lawn. The president signaled Julie Nixon Eisenhower with a thumbs-up. She returned the gesture and tried not to cry.

Then the helicopter lifted President Richard Nixon off the White House lawn for the last time.

CHAPTER ELEVEN

From Exile to Elder Statesman

ONE MONTH LATER President Gerald Ford granted Richard Nixon a pardon for his role in Watergate. The American people were outraged. Ford's popularity in the opinion polls dropped twenty-two points overnight, the largest single loss ever recorded. The Gallup poll showed that 62 percent of Americans were against pardoning the former president, as opposed to 31 percent in favor. Upon taking office Ford had characterized the tormented last year and a half of the Nixon administration as "our long national nightmare." In praising the Constitution he had said, "Our great republic is a government of laws and not of men. Here the people rule." About his predecessor he noted, "May our president who brought peace to millions find it for himself."

But Richard Nixon remained a troubled man. As he walked the grounds of his Pacific coast estate in San Clemente alone, he was haunted by memories of his own mistakes. Although he had no job, Nixon tried to resume a normal working routine as quickly as possible, showing up at his office in a suit and tie at 7:00 A.M. He was irritated when his loyal staff of former White House aides did not show up punctually at 7:30, and he glowered when one young man turned up for a meeting in Bermuda shorts. One morning at a staff meeting he said, "I've called you here to discuss an important topic. And that is, what are we going to do about the economy in the coming year?"[1]

If it seemed absurd for Nixon the private citizen to behave as if he were still running the country, it was not absurd for him to be concerned about his personal economic status. After paying back taxes of hundreds of thousands of dollars he was practically broke. He decided to write his memoirs, calling in super-agent Swifty Lazar to negotiate a publishing deal. Lazar told him he could probably get a $2 million advance, but only if he was honest in writing about Watergate. Or, he told Nixon, there was another way that he could earn even more money.

"What's that?" asked Nixon.

"Leave your body to the Harvard Medical School," Lazar quipped.

As his loyal aides headed to prison, Nixon got $2.5 million from Warner Books to write his version of recent history. But even with his financial problems temporarily solved he continued to be moody, depressed, and unable to concentrate for extended periods of time. Even the pardon had not helped to lift his spirits, and Nixon went so far as to call President Ford and offer to give it back, claiming that he was concerned about Ford's reputation. On top of his emotional problems Nixon had recurring phlebitis, an inflammation of the veins. It had flared up on his 1974 trips to the Middle East and the Soviet Union, but Nixon had managed to soldier through his itineraries.

When it flared up in California his doctor insisted that he be hospitalized. It turned out that the clot in his leg had broken free and could have killed Nixon had it traveled to his brain. He was released from the hospital quickly, but before long he was back in intensive care. One of the large veins leading to his heart was "99^{44}/$_{100}$ percent blocked." At one point, Nixon went into shock and had to be revived. Later he described hearing the nurse say, "Richard, pull yourself back." It was then that he realized that he had to choose which way he would go. And, as many people have reported when describing near-death experiences, Nixon related how he knew that it was not his time to go. He had more work to do in this lifetime. He returned to consciousness with a new insight about the nature of his life and a new sympathy for others who had described similar experiences.

President Ford was concerned about Nixon, but his advisers told him not to pay a hospital visit, warning that it would be politically risky to do so. But Ford said, "If there's no place in politics for human compassion, there's something wrong with politics." He called Pat Nixon and asked whether it would be helpful if he stopped in to see Nixon.

"I can't think of anything that would do him more good," Pat replied.

When Ford entered the intensive care unit, he noticed how frail Nixon seemed. His speech was slurred, and when Ford asked him how his nights were, Nixon answered, "None of my nights are too good." Ford touched Nixon's hand reassuringly. The bedridden man said, "Mr. President, this has meant a lot to me. I'm deeply grateful." Leaving the hospital, Ford thought it might be the last time he saw Richard Nixon alive.

Shortly afterward Nixon's left lung began to fill with fluid and he developed pneumonia. He could hardly walk and his blood count was low. But he managed to pull through sufficiently to be discharged a few weeks later. When he got home Pat nursed him back to health, preparing his meals and making sure that he ate when he needed to. Nixon acknowledged her devotion, saying, "I doubt I would have made it without her." It was Pat who organized a surprise birthday party when Nixon turned sixty-two. Even though she knew he hated birthdays, she thought it would be good for him to have his friends around. He was genuinely pleased when they showed up, and he was genuinely surprised. He had also been surprised to get a birthday note from Chinese leader Zhou Enlai and a phone call from President Ford. As he offered a toast to his friends, his eyes teared. "Never dwell on the past. Always look to the future." One of his friends noticed how Nixon, at one time the most powerful man in the world, had become vulnerable and isolated.

He showed a bit of his former feistiness when he told Senator Barry Goldwater that he looked forward to a time when Watergate would be a faded image from the past. Then he, Nixon, could reemerge as a spokesman for the Republican party or perhaps even an ambassador to China. At least that was Goldwater's version. When the story hit the newspapers the next day Nixon denied having said that at all. "Christ, I know how the American public would never accept a thing like that. There may be a few million hard-core Nixonites out there, but there are hundreds of millions of others who are anti-Nixon. I know that."

Among those "hard-core Nixonites" was Rabbi Korff, who was running a campaign to get the White House to stop "harassing" Nixon. At issue were hundreds of thousands of presidential documents and letters that the government was refusing to release to him. Among them were memos on the president's brother Donald's phone being tapped; Nixon's enemies in the media; some horoscopes; and suggestions on how to get more mileage out of the glamour of the White House. Pat Nixon's inaugural gown and Julie's wedding dress were among the personal items impounded. To Rabbi Korff withholding these items was tantamount to robbing Nixon of his "last vestige of dignity." It was emasculating to the former president, whom he described as "tormented" and in poor "physical and emotional health." What's more, Korff said, Nixon had "deep regrets, profound regrets" about Watergate. Nixon was not pleased by Korff's apology on his behalf. But when a Quaker pastor from Whittier paid him a call Nixon conceded, "There was some wrong in what I did. I made a big mistake." Several weeks later he reversed himself again, blaming his problems on H. R. Haldeman, who was serving an eighteen-month prison sentence. "This Watergate thing was ridiculous. Nothing like the press made it out to be," Nixon said. On another ocassion he startled a former CIA official by asking, "What did I do wrong?"

While his sentiments about Watergate were vacillating, his finances were again dwindling. At one point Nixon had only $500 in his checking account. He was paying off more than $400,000 in federal back taxes discovered by the Internal Revenue Service during the Watergate investigation. He could no longer afford the upkeep on his Pacific estate and he and Pat were grateful when a local Boy Scout troop volunteered to help with the lawns. The sign outside his house, which used to read Avenieda El Presidente, had been changed to read Avenieda Ex El Presidente. And the Nixon estate was so run-down that his neighbors complained that Ex El Presidente was hurting their property values.

Despite his tremendous book advance, Nixon was hard-pressed for cash and in the summer of 1975 negotiated a $600,000 fee with British television personality and producer David Frost for a series of interviews that would include a no-holds-barred discussion of Watergate. That may have marked a turning point for Richard Nixon; the rest of the summer saw him slowly emerging from what one of his aides called "exile." His concentration improved and he was able to work on his memoirs for longer periods of time. He began to communicate with Mao Zedong, Leonid Brezhnev, and the Shah of Iran. He hung giant pictures of himself with Chinese leaders in his office as reminders of his greatest triumph. During his stay in the hospital Mao Zedong had phoned him to say that Richard Nixon was "one of the greatest statesmen in history." Nixon also got back in touch with several foreign ambassadors and spoke more regularly with President Ford. He began getting phone calls from Henry Kissinger, who wanted Nixon to commiserate about the trials of conducting foreign policy in the Ford administration. Kissinger called Nixon from a plane in which he was shuttling from one Middle Eastern nation to another. He told Nixon that he was going to resign. Nixon rolled his eyes and said, "Now, now Henry. The country needs you." When he got off the phone he said, "There are two ways of handling Henry. Sometimes you've got to pat him on the head. And sometimes you've got to kick him right in the nuts."[2] If that was vintage Richard Nixon, so was the resurgence of his fighting spirit. "Our day will come again," he predicted to a friend. And when John Wayne gave him a horse sculpture and praised him for holding on during "that rough ride in Washington," Nixon grinned. "One day this horse may gallop again."

In February 1976 Nixon returned to China for the first of many visits as a private citizen. As he had during his 1972 trip, he made headlines. Not all of them were flattering. Nixon had promised Gerald Ford that he would not do anything that would hurt Ford's chances of winning the 1976 election. Ford was still smarting from the public response to his pardoning of Nixon and he was not pleased to be upstaged by Nixon's trip. Senator Goldwater said that if Nixon wanted to do the country a favor, "he might stay over there." Columnists denounced the trip as "a sleazy act," the kind of deed that first earned him the nickname Tricky Dick. Mary McGrory of the *Washington Star* wrote, "Sure, Gerald Ford spared him indictment, trial, possible prison. . . . But what has he done for [Nixon] lately?"

If public opinion was hostile in his own country, in the People's Republic of China Richard Nixon was cheered as a returning hero. Everywhere he went people turned out to chant his name. He was treated to a sumptuous banquet and top-level meetings, much as he had been when he was president. When he presented his toast at the end of a state banquet, Nixon sounded as if he *were* still president. "There is much work to be done. But we are determined to complete it," he said.

When he returned to the United States the Ford administration backed down from its position that the former president had simply gone to China as a "private citizen." His visit had been too important for them to ignore, and Kissinger asked his former boss to brief him on the trip. Nixon relished this turn of events. It was definitive proof that he was making yet another political comeback. "I don't intend to just fade away," said Nixon of his second wind. "I intend to continue to do everything that I can in my new position, that of being not in political life but in public life, of attempting to continue to speak out on issues that may affect the peace of the world." He might have retired from politics, but Richard Nixon certainly had not retired from public life.

It wasn't long before he was secretly contacted by an adviser to President Gerald Ford, who was now running in the Republican primaries. Ford needed Nixon's help, and soon the former president was engaged as a confidential source to the White House. Code-named "the Wizard" by White House staffers, Richard Nixon was a fountain of information. And many of his suggestions brought back memories of those mean, suspicious off-the-cuff remarks that his secret taping system had captured while he was president. Don't get friendly with your Secret Service agents, Nixon told Ford. "The minute you start getting familiar with people, they start taking advantage." And watch out for Nancy Reagan, he warned about the future First Lady, "Nancy Reagan's a bitch, and Ronnie [Ford's chief rival for the Republican nomination] listens to her." Kissinger angered him when he made several speeches about emerging African nations. "It's pissing off the rednecks," Nixon said. "The Negro vote's lost. The Democrats have Negroes and the Jews. And let them have them. In fact, tie them around their necks."

With regard to the upcoming election between Ford and Jimmy Carter, the Democratic nominee for the presidency, Nixon told Ford to attack the liberal foreign policy stance. "Carter scares the hell out of me. He'll come close to making us a number-two power." Nixon further pushed Ford to use those fears to scare the American people. And, he said, make sure one of your own television consultants is in the control room whenever you appear on camera so that no technician with Democratic sensibilities can undermine you by choosing unflattering shots. Most important, Nixon insisted that "Wizard" or not, he remain behind the scenes, totally incognito. Ford should not let people know that Nixon was helping him. "Don't worry what you say about Nixon," he informed Ford. "Murder me. I understand."[3]

Even with his association with Nixon hidden from the public, Ford lost the 1976 presidential election by two percentage points. Many people said that they didn't vote for him because he had pardoned Nixon. But when Ford was asked whether he would do it again, he said he thought he still would have.

While secretly advising Ford during the campaign, Nixon had been preoccupied because Pat had suffered a stroke a few months earlier while reading Bob Woodward and Carl Bernstein's book *The Final Days*. Apparently the book's intimate descriptions of their marriage and of her husband's secret drinking were shattering to her. Nixon was furious at the authors, but full of praise for Pat's fighting spirit. "She is not giving up," he said.

Pat's stroke caused him to postpone the taping of his interviews with David Frost, and when the two men finally sat down to talk on March 23, 1977, it was more than a year after the signing of their agreement. Frost was concerned about the delay and feared that it would mean that the show would not be scheduled until the following August, the month when television ratings are at their lowest. Nixon told him not to worry. "We got a helluva rating August 9, 1974."

"Yes, but what do you do for an encore?" Frost shot back.

Glib and evasive during their first few interviews, Nixon slithered around Frost's questions by rambling on about the political leaders he had known. Questioned about his resignation, Nixon suddenly gave viewers a rare look at his feelings. "Resignation meant life without purpose so far as I was concerned. Life without purpose . . . could be a very, very shattering experience, which it has been. And . . . to a certain extent, still is. No one in the world, and no one in our history, could know how I felt. No one can know how it feels to resign the presidency of the United States. Isn't that punishment enough? Oh, probably not," said Nixon, adding that although he didn't know what the future would bring, he would "still be fighting." He confessed that he had wanted to end the Vietnam War and he blamed it on Kennedy and Johnson. "They got us in. They sent the men over there, I didn't," he insisted.

Frost was frustrated with Nixon's evasion of the issues on which he had wanted to pin him down, but the television crew was charmed. "If that guy runs for president again, I'm going to vote for him," one cameraman said.

The climax of the series of interviews was Nixon's discussion of his role in Watergate. After all, that was what he had been paid $600,000 to talk about. Frost went on the offensive, telling Nixon that the American people wanted to hear him apologize for the years of agony he had put them through. Nixon waffled at first, defending his record on foreign policy and blaming the "partisan" Congress and media for his downfull. But he admitted that he would have been "crippled" by a full Senate trial following the impeachment votes and he conceded, "I have impeached myself. By resigning. That was voluntary impeachment." His eyes closed, Nixon recalled those last days in office. "I sort of cracked up, started to cry. Then I blurted it out. I said, 'I'm sorry. I just hope I haven't let you down.' Well, when I said 'I just hope I haven't let you down' I said it all. I had. I let down my friends. I let down the country. I let down our system of government. Dreams of all those young people that are thinking that government is all too corrupt and the rest. Yup. I let the American people down. And I have to carry that burden with me for the rest of my life. My political life is over."

His apology, which was watched by fifty million Americans on May 4, 1977, failed to convince many people. After all, Nixon was still gallivanting around the world being quoted in the news.

Several months later his political colleagues were in a conciliatory mood, welcoming him back when he flew to Washington to attend Hubert Humphrey's funeral. He joshed with Henry Kissinger, asking him if he was as mean as ever, and compared golf scores with Gerald Ford. Despite an occasional glance back over his shoulder at the trials of Watergate, Richard Nixon definitely kept his eye on an active future. "I'm not just going to fade away and live the good life in San Clemente, listening to the waves and playing golf," he said. "If I did that I would be dead mentally in a year, and physically, too."

Having whipped himself back into fighting shape, Richard Nixon was in the market for a more challenging environment. He began making jokes about San Clemente, claiming that you had to be seventy-two years old to live there. He gave away his golf clubs. In 1980 he and Pat finally moved to a townhouse in New York City. (They had been turned down by two co-op boards as undesirables.) Nixon loved New York. "Any town that supports the Mets is always for the underdog," he joked. But the polls on Nixon were already beginning to show that the president who had resigned in disgrace was no longer considered an underdog. In fact a 1978 Gallup poll voted Richard Nixon among the top ten people whom Americans most admired. Two years earlier another Gallup poll had found him to be one of the most hated.

Nixon's new, relaxed sense of himself was partly due to the birth of his two grandchildren, Tricia's son, Christopher, and Julie's daughter, Jennie. When Julie asked her father what he wanted the baby to call him, he had said in typically dry Nixon fashion, "Well, R.N. would be nice." But when the baby was able to make sounds, she called him "Ba" and the name stuck. All his grandchildren call him "Ba."

It seemed that Nixon was becoming more comfortable with children in general. When one of his former aides from San Clemente brought her nephew and two of his friends to get the former president's autograph, he spent two hours talking to them and served them milk and cookies.

By 1982, however, Nixon was restless and looking for a new place to live. He had come back to his townhouse one afternoon to find some school girls from the Catholic elementary school across the street sitting on his front step smoking marijuana. Saying that he did not want his grandchildren exposed to such shenanigans, he purchased a four-and-a-half-acre estate in Upper Saddle River, New Jersey. With its spacious grounds and tennis court, it afforded the Nixons some privacy but was still within one hour of New York City, where Nixon had his office.

For the first time in his life Richard Nixon seemed at peace with himself and his world. Although he remained as undemonstrative as ever, he and Pat were closer than they had ever been in all their years of marriage. More than ever he was glad that he had not listened when Haldeman had suggested that he divorce Pat because she was a political liability. Looking to the future, Richard Nixon predicted that in another couple of generations, nobody would remember Watergate. Rather, he would be known in history as a great statesman. Nixon received confirmation of his self-assessment from none other than his former political opponent George McGovern, who read Nixon's book *Leaders,* which was published in 1982, and wrote him a note that said, "History will remember you as one of the great peacemakers of the twentieth century."

Another chance to return to the role of statesman opened up for Nixon in October 1981, when Egyptian president Anwar Sadat was assassinated. President Ronald Reagan sent former presidents Gerald Ford, Jimmy Carter, and Richard

Nixon to Sadat's funeral. When an official photographer wanted the three former presidents to pose, Nixon stepped aside, flushing. "You don't want my picture with them," he said. But the photographer insisted and as he stood in the middle with his arms around Ford's and Carter's waists, Richard Nixon grinned. He was accepted as their peer.

Back home a band played "Hail to the Chief" when he spoke at a thousand-dollar-a-plate Republican banquet. Richard Nixon had been introduced as "truly one of our great presidents." When he traveled to Morocco in 1982 seventy-five thousand people gathered to cheer him. Some carried signs that said YOU SHOULD STILL BE PRESIDENT. And there were endless interviews. Facing off with his former assistant Diane Sawyer, who had become a CBS News anchorwoman, Nixon conceded that he should have burned the tapes to begin with. In fact his wife had urged him to do that at the time. The secret of his renewed success? In 1982 he told Sawyer that it was "never looking back." He insisted that Watergate was already a few paragraphs in the history books. In fifty years it would be a footnote.

Forgive and forget appeared to be Nixon's motto when it came to Watergate. Although he predicted that Watergate would become a footnote with the passing of time, he knew he really could not write that final chapter. Writing about Watergate and his presidency in his *Memoirs*, Richard Nixon observed, "History will make the final judgment. It is a judgment I do not fear."

Epilogue

EXCHANGING TOASTS WITH Chinese leaders in the fall of 1989 during another successful trip to the People's Republic of China, Richard Nixon said that the administration of George Bush should follow the path that he started during his first triumphant visit to China in 1972.

His seventh book, *1999: Victory without War*, was published earlier in 1989. Nixon described it as the product of "a lifetime of study and on-the-job training in foreign policy." Calling for a global perspective on events in the coming century, Nixon predicted in *1999* that the competition between the United States and the Soviet Union will continue to dominate the world stage, but emphasized that American leaders will have to develop policies that enable China, Japan, and Western Europe to play a larger role. "In 1999, we will remember the twentieth century as the bloodiest and best in the history of man. The twentieth century will be remembered as a century of war and wonder. We must make the twenty-first a century of peace."

Although he claimed to have put Watergate behind him, Richard Nixon has been quick to flare up when the subject has received a public airing. When AT&T decided to sponsor a docudrama of Woodward and Bernstein's book *The Final Days* that was broadcast on ABC-TV in October 1989, Nixon switched his telephone service from AT&T to MCI and refused to do any interviews for ABC News.

It seemed particularly fitting when Nixon won an award for his fund-raising efforts on behalf of a French school recently. The other award recipients were the Surrealist artist Salvador Dali and Federico Fellini, a director whose films are frequently surrealistic. To those who lived through the chilling years of Nixon's wiretapping and Vietnam War policy, his political resurrection is nothing if not surreal. Bob Woodward, whose Watergate reporting helped bring down the Nixon presidency, deems "the so-called comeback of Richard Nixon an assault on history and our democratic values." He points out that although Nixon referred to the Watergate break-in as "a little thing," it was not an isolated incident. The Nixon White House had been conducting illegal surveillance projects for years. Woodward noted that "the Watergate break-in was merely the loose thread that unraveled the sock."

Although he has been praised for his foreign policy accomplishments, it was Richard Nixon who conspired with Henry Kissinger to raise covert foreign policy to a high art. The Iran-Contra scandal in which the Reagan White House was accused of illegally diverting funds to aid the antigovernment forces in Nicaragua in the 1980s was an illegitimate godchild of Richard Nixon's.

The cartoonist Jules Feiffer, who has caricatured Richard Nixon for years, sums him up as "a great American counterhero, the godfather of sleaze." Feiffer gives Nixon points for endurance, saying, "He has been in a prominent position on the political stage since 1948." He also credits Nixon for being "brilliant at reinventing himself," saying, "You have to admire the snake's refusal to die." (As one recent cartoon puts it: Reagan is history. Nixon is forever.)

There is no doubt that Richard Nixon is both indomitable and fiercely intelligent. Many believe him to be the most intelligent president of this century. If nothing else, his hard work and persistence deserve a certain grudging admiration.

But consider the following:

Fact: As president, Richard Nixon committed criminal acts.

Fact: He lied about those acts as he had lied about his opponents in order to get elected.

Fact: He resigned in disgrace.

Fact: To have done otherwise may still have resulted in his impeachment.

Ignorance is bad enough. To insist on remaining ignorant by refusing to recognize the truth is downright dangerous. Thomas Finnegan, a twelve-year-old honor student from East Atlantic Beach, New York, read some of this manuscript as I was working on it. "When you write the end of your biography of Richard Nixon," he told me, "you need to quote the Duke of Attenborough and Winston Churchill: 'He who doesn't read history is bound to repeat it.' "

Notes

Unless otherwise noted, quotations and references are taken from Stephen Ambrose's *Nixon Volume I: The Education of a Politician 1913–1962* (New York: Simon & Schuster, 1987). Ambrose synthesizes material from several other Nixon biographies, and many of these quotations are cross-referenced.

Chapter One: The Early Years

1. Nixon's description of his grandmother appears in Ambrose, p. 11.
2. The canal incident appears on p. 23.

3. Frank's reference to Hannah's quiet discipline appears on p. 24.

4. Nixon's reference to the sound of the train appears on p. 26.

5. The quotation about Nixon's "becoming a lawyer they can't bribe" appears on p. 27.

6. The reference to Nixon's avoiding argumentative people appears on p. 37.

7. The famous letter signed "Your good dog, Richard" appears on p. 37.

8. Nixon's quotation about the "starts and slights and snubs" of his childhood appears on p. 39.

9. His reference to feeling sorry for the guy who has to pick rotten apples out of the pile appears on p. 43.

10. The reference to his first political opponent in high school appears on p. 49.

11. The campus newspaper column is quoted on p. 63.

12. Nixon describes himself as "relatively shy" on p. 83.

13. Pat Nixon's quotation about thinking that Richard was "nuts or something" appears on p. 93.

14. Pat's description of life as "sort of sad" appears on p. 95.

15. Nixon's farewell dinner with his family is described on p. 107.

16. The quotation about Nixon not wanting to reveal himself appears on p. 114.

17. Admiral Spruance's quotation and the navy citation appear on p. 115.

Chapter Two: The Alger Hiss Case

1. Pat's conditions about campaigning appear on p. 118.

2. Nixon's former classmate comments on his transformation on p. 36.

3. Nixon quotation about Voorhis appears on p. 140.

4. Ambrose quotation on Nixon profiting from HUAC appears on p. 152.

5. Nixon discusses Hiss with his mother on p. 176.

6. Nixon's and Chambers's comments during the microfilm incident appear on p. 193.

Chapter Three: Tricky Dick

1. Kennedy's contribution to Nixon's campaign appears on p. 211.

2. Pat describes feeling guilty about leaving her daughters with baby-sitters on p. 244.

3. Nixon's reverence for Eisenhower and Eisenhower's praise for Nixon appear on p. 232.

4. The reference to Nixon being called "a little man in a big hurry" is taken from notes that I used to compile his obituary for CBS News.

5. Tricia's comment about campaigning appears on p. 267.

Chapter Four: Checkers

1. *Sacramento Bee* reference to Nixon's being the "pet and protégé" of rich businessmen appears on p. 277.

2. Nixon's quotation about "crooks and communism" appears on p. 279.

3. Nixon's famous quotation about Pat's "Republican cloth coat" appears on p. 281.

4. Eisenhower's quotation about not wanting to condemn an innocent man and Nixon's response appear on p. 282.

Chapter Five: Riding This Great Stream of History

1. The "famous so-called Chicken Lunch" is described on p. 333.

2. Nixon talks about secretly recording Eisenhower on p. 334.

3. McCarthy says he is "sick and tired" of "that prick Nixon" on p. 338.

4. Nixon's quotation on "the only way to deal with communism" appears on p. 325.

5. Operation Vulture is described on p. 343.

6. The quotations about the Nixons and their social lives and appearances appear on p. 350.

7. Nixon's doctor is mentioned on p. 351.

8. Nixon's comments upon hearing about Eisenhower's heart attack appear on p. 371.

9. Reference to Eisenhower's calling Nixon "a darn good young man" and comments on his immaturity appear on p. 377.

10. Nixon calls Eisenhower a "complex and devious man" in his *Memoirs*. The quotation appears on p. 382.

11. The quotation about "this great stream of history" is taken from Earl Mazo and Stephen Hess's *Richard Nixon: A Personal and Political Portrait* (New York: Avon Books, 1960), p. 157.

Chapter Six: You Won't Have Richard Nixon to Kick Around Anymore

1. Eisenhower's praises of Nixon and his suggestion to "give 'em heaven" appear on pp. 410 and 411.

2. Nixon's remark about the administration and Chotiner appears on p. 398.

3. Nixon's description of his letdown after crisis appears on p. 479.

4. Eisenhower's quotation, "If you gave me a week I might think of something," appears on p. 559.

5. Theodore White's description of Nixon as looking pasty is from his book *The Making of the President, 1960* (New York: Atheneum, 1961). The quote also appears on p. 571 of the Ambrose biography.

6. Meg Greenfield in the *Reporter* magazine used the phrase "leadership by association." It also appears on p. 569 of Ambrose.

7. Kennedy's affairs are discussed on p. 585.

8. Tricia's disappointment when her father loses the election appears on p. 605.

9. Nixon's decision not to demand a recount is described on p. 606.

10. The discussion of people's approval of a discrimination clause in Nixon's lease appears on p. 661 and Pat Nixon's comment about smears appears on p. 666.

11. Nixon compares losing the California governorship to being stung by a mosquito on p. 669.

Chapter Seven: The New Nixon

1. Nixon's belief that he would challenge Kennedy in 1964 is discussed in Herbert S. Parmet's *Richard Nixon and His America* (Boston: Little, Brown, 1990), p. 438.

2. Nixon's civil rights speech in Cincinnati appears in Parmet, p. 445.

3. Nixon's views on Vietnam appear in Parmet, p. 452.

4. Abbie Hoffman was quoted in his obituary, CBS Evening News, April 13, 1989.

5. Nixon's article in *Foreign Affairs* is quoted in Parmet, p. 496.

6. Eugene McCarthy gave the monthly estimate of how much the Vietnam War was costing on November 30, 1967. He is quoted in Charles Kaiser's *1968 in America: Music, Politics, Chaos, Counterculture, and the Shaping of a Generation* (New York: Weidenfeld & Nicolson, 1988).

7. Tet statistics are quoted in Kaiser, p. 79.

8. King's quotation about not fearing death appears in Kaiser, p. 210.

9. Humphrey talks about Nixon's "political face-lifts" in Kaiser, p. 226.

10. The discussion of CIA, FBI, and Daley's security forces at the Chicago convention and the description of the events outside the convention hall are drawn from Kaiser, pp. 230–244.

11. Humphrey's defense of Daley's actions at the Democratic National Convention appear in Kaiser, p. 241.

12. Lyndon Johnson's warning to Humphrey is recounted in Kaiser, p. 249.

13. The details of Nixon's media campaign come from Joe

McGinniss's *Selling of the President 1968* (New York: Pocket Books, 1970). Nixon is described as "raising the platitude to an art form" in McGinniss, p. 118.

Chapter Eight: The Presidency

1. Nixon's remarks about Jews are reported in *The Price of Power*, Seymour M. Hersh (New York: Summit Books, 1983), p. 84. Kissinger's comments about anti-Semitism in the White House appear on p. 603. Nixon's racist comments appear on p. 110.

2. Kissinger's secret diary is described in Hersh, p. 108. The concerns of Nixon's aides for the nation's safety are described in Hersh, p. 109.

3. Kissinger's discussion of wiretapping with J. Edgar Hoover is recounted in Hersh, p. 87.

4. Kissinger's decision to wiretap four of his Jewish aides in order to appeal to the anti-Semitism in the Oval Office and Nixon's comment about being uncomfortable with Kissinger's wiretapping are described in Hersh, pp. 91–94.

5. The quotation about Kissinger's keeping Haig around so that he would have someone to testify on his behalf at a war crimes trial and Haig's comments about Kissinger's masturbating in his office appear in Hersh, pp. 115–116.

6. The account of Nixon's secretly taping Kissinger is reported in Hersh, p. 316.

7. Kissinger's talking about retrieving documents and the account of Kissinger at the secret meeting appear in Hersh, pp. 383–384.

Chapter Nine: Watergate

1. Nixon's statement that the White House had no involvement with the Watergate break-in and Mitchell's comments appear in Bob Woodward and Carl Bernstein's *All the President's Men* (New York: Simon & Schuster, 1974), p. 28.

2. McGovern compared Nixon to Hitler in various press reports. The quotation is taken from the 1989 TV documentary *Richard Nixon: The Untold Story* produced by Barbara Howar.

3. Pat's misgivings about the reelection campaign are mentioned in Julie Nixon Eisenhower's *Pat Nixon: The Untold Story* (New York: Simon & Schuster, 1986), p. 348.

4. Nixon's melancholy response to his reelection is described in Eisenhower, p. 352.

5. Haldeman's suggestion that Nixon divorce his wife is recounted in Robert S. Anson's *Exile* (New York: Simon & Schuster, 1984).

6. Larry O'Brien's quotation about the "bungled" burglary appears in Woodward and Bernstein, *All the President's Men*, p. 26.

7. Rose Mary Woods says "For once, Henry, behave like a man" on p. 32 of Bob Woodward and Carl Bernstein's *Final Days* (New York: Simon & Schuster, 1976).

8. Nixon's feeling superior to Kennedy because of Kennedy's involvement with Marilyn Monroe is described in Woodward and Bernstein, *Final Days*, pp. 51–53.

9. Nixon is quoted as saying "Brezhnev wouldn't understand" in Woodward and Bernstein, *Final Days*, p. 70.

10. Nixon proposes making a new Dictabelt of a private Oval Office meeting in Woodward and Bernstein, *Final Days*, p. 27.

Chapter Ten: The Final Days

1. Nixon's drinking and mood swings are described in Woodward and Bernstein, *Final Days*, p. 104.

2. David Eisenhower's expression of his fears that Nixon may be "going bananas" and his description of Nixon's eyes as appearing glazed and tranquilized are in Woodward and Bernstein, *Final Days*, pp. 343 and 347.

3. Julie tells Pat about Nixon's decision to resign in Eisenhower, p. 418.

4. Buchanan talks about Nixon's misleading the American public in Woodward and Bernstein, *Final Days*, p. 319.

5. Cox's account of Nixon's talking to the pictures on the wall in the White House appears in Woodward and Bernstein, *Final Days*, p. 395.

6. Nixon's comment to Haig about "a pistol in a drawer" and Haig's comparison of Nixon to Captain Queeg appear in Woodward and Bernstein, *Final Days*, pp. 403–404.

7. Kissinger's belief that Nixon was mentally incapacitated is discussed in Woodward and Bernstein, *Final Days*, p. 189, and Kissinger's description of the scene with Nixon in the Lincoln Sitting Room as "the most wrenching thing" appears on p. 424.

8. The description of Pat Nixon's speaking to Nixon appears in Anson, p. 87.

Chapter Eleven: From Exile to Elder Statesman

1. Nixon's return to a normal working routine and the description of his meeting after leaving the White House are described in Anson, p. 30.

2. Nixon talks about "two ways of handling Henry [Kissinger]" in Anson, p. 116.

3. See Anson, pp. 143–150 and pp. 222–239. Specifically Nixon offers advice to Ford on p. 144; talks about Negroes and Jews on p. 148; and offers Ford advice on using television on p. 148.

Select Bibliography

Ambrose, Stephen E. *Nixon: The Education of a Politician, 1913–1962*, Vol. I. New York: Simon & Schuster, 1987.

Ambrose, Stephen E. *Nixon, The Triumph of a Politician, 1962–1972*, Vol II. New York: Simon & Schuster, 1981.

Anson, Robert. *Exile: The Unquite Oblivion of Richard M. Nixon*. New York: Simon & Schuster, 1984.

Branch, Taylor. *Parting the Waters: America in the King Years 1954–63*. New York: Simon & Schuster, 1988.

Crouse, Timothy. *The Boys on the Bus: Riding with the Campaign Press Corps*. New York: Ballantine Books, 1972.

Eisenhower, Julie Nixon. *Pat Nixon: The Untold Story*. New York: Simon & Schuster, 1986.

Gardner, Gerald. *The Mocking of the President: A History of Campaign Humor from Ike to Bush.* Detroit: Wayne State University Press, 1989.

Hersh, Seymour M. *The Price of Power: Kissinger in the Nixon White House.* New York: Summit Books, 1983.

Kaiser, Charles *1968 in America: Music, Politics, Chaos, Counterculture, and the Shaping of a Generation.* New York: Weidenfeld & Nicolson, 1988.

Mazo, Earl, and Stephen Hess. *Nixon: A Personal and Political Portrait.* New York: Avon Books, 1962.

McGinniss, Joe. *The Selling of the President 1968.* New York: Pocket Books, 1970.

Morris, Roger. *Richard Milhous Nixon: The Rise of an American Politician.* New York: Henry Holt, 1990.

Nixon, Richard M. *RN: The Memoirs of Richard Nixon.* New York: Grosset and Dunlap, 1978.

Nixon, Richard M. *In the Arena: A Memoir of Victory, Defeat, and Renewal.* New York: Simon & Schuster, 1990.

Nixon, Richard M. *1999: Victory Without War.* New York: Simon & Schuster, 1988.

Oudes, Bruce, ed. *From the President: Richard Nixon's Secret Files*, New York: Harper and Row, 1989.

Parmet, Herbert S. *Richard Nixon and His America.* Boston: Little Brown, 1990.

Rather, Dan, and Gary Paul Gates. *The Palace Guard.* New York: Harper and Row, 1974.

Schell, Jonathan. *Observing the Nixon Years.* New York: Random House, 1989.

Sirica, John J. *To Set the Record Straight: The Break-in, the Tapes, the Conspirators, the Pardon.* New York: New American Library, 1979.

Sulzberger, C. L. *The World and Richard Nixon*. New York: Prentice Hall Press, 1987.

Washington Post, ed. *The Presidential Transcripts*. New York: Delacorte Press, 1974.

White, Theodore H. *The Making of the President, 1960*. New York: Atheneum, 1961.

White, Theodore H. *The Making of the President, 1968*. New York: Atheneum, 1969.

White, Theodore H. *The Making of the President, 1972*. New York: Atheneum, 1973.

Winship, Michael. *Television*. New York: Random House, 1988.

Woodward, Bob, and Carl Bernstein. *All the President's Men*. New York: Simon & Schuster, 1974.

Woodward, Bob, and Carl Bernstein. *The Final Days*. New York: Simon & Schuster, 1976.

Index

Quaker religion, 3, 4, 5, 6, 10–11,
14, 25, 39, 176, 184

racial bias, 101, 132–133, 187
racial violence, 107, 111–112,
117, 120
Rather, Dan, 122, 128–129, 140,
144, 166, 168
Reagan, Nancy, 187
Reagan, Ronald, 35, 49, 192
Rebozo, Bebe, 134, 160, 167, 171,
172
Republican National Committee, 62
resignation from presidency, 164,
166, 168, 171–175, 176–
178
Richardson, Elliott, 162, 163
Rogers, William, 132
Roosevelt, Franklin Delano, 31, 38,
49, 131, 141
Rubin, Jerry, 111
Ruckelshaus, William, 163
Ryan, Thelma Catherine (Pat),
(wife), 26, 28, 29, 42, 43,
44, 53–54, 57, 60–61, 62,
63, 85, 97, 98, 99, 141,
182, 183, 192, 193
election campaigns, assisting in,
33, 58, 59, 101
consideration of others, 21–23
courtship, 23–24
education, 22–23
first meeting, 21
growing up, 22
political life, dislike of, 30, 51–
52, 65, 74–75, 89, 113
public image, 95–96
South America trip, 82–88

self-denial, 21–22
stroke, suffering, 188
teaching career, 23
Watergate scandal, 152, 153,
172, 177–178
wedding and honeymoon, 24

Sadat, Anwar, 192
St. Patrick's Cathedral, 118
SALT talks, 146
San Clemente, California, 156,
180, 191
San Diego Union, 82
"Saturday Night Massacre," 163,
168
Sawyer, Diane, 168, 193
Screen Actors Guild, 49
screenwriters, HUAC attacks on, 35
secrecy, obsession with, 129, 134,
141–142, 143, 147
Senate Democratic Caucus, 153
Senate Foreign Relations Commit-
tee, 136
Senate Judiciary Committee, 164
Senate Subcommittee on Privileges
and Elections, 64
Senate Watergate Committee, 154,
160, 171
Shah of Iran, 185
Sheehan, Neil, 142–143
Sihanouk, Prince, 135
Silent Majority, 138, 139
Sirhan, Sirhan, 118, 119
Sirica, Judge, 162, 164
Six Crises, writing of, 99–100
Smith, Hedrick, 143
social welfare issues, 31, 49, 94,
109